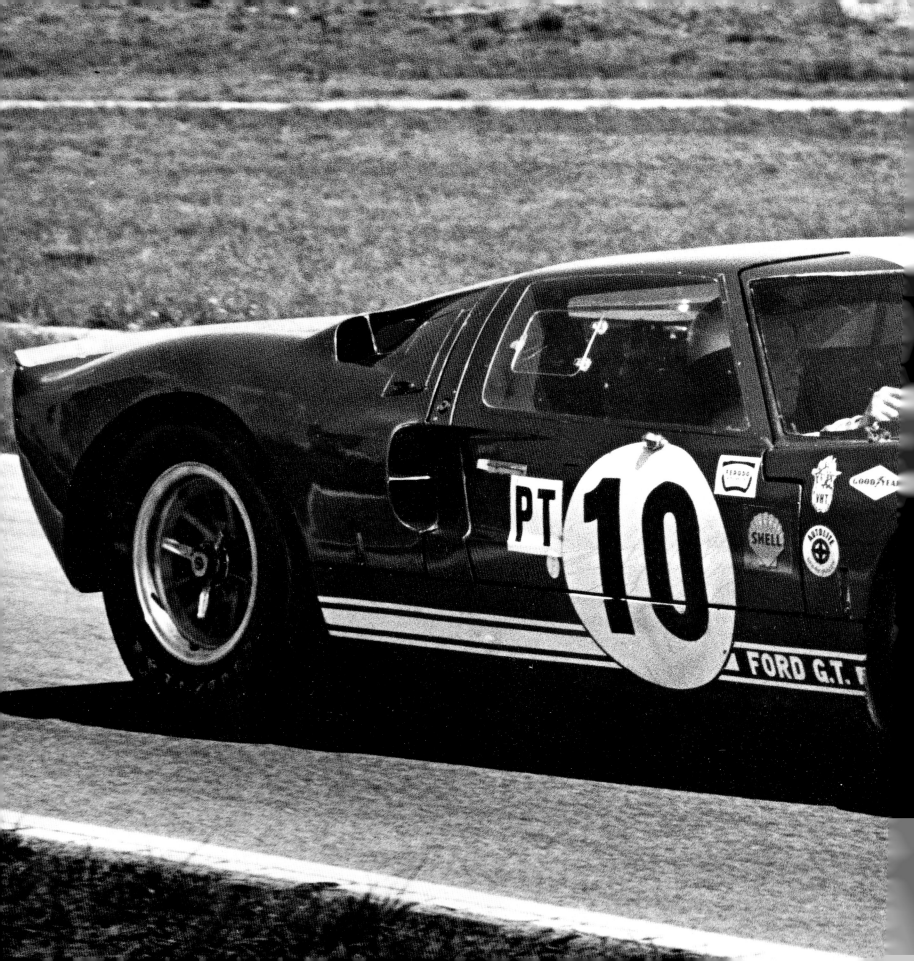

SHELBY GT40

Dave Friedman

Motorbooks International
Publishers & Wholesalers

First published in 1995 by Motorbooks International Publishers & Wholesalers, PO Box 2, 729 Prospect Avenue, Osceola, WI 54020 USA

Motorbooks International books are also available at discounts in bulk quantity for industrial or sales-promotional use. For details write to Special Sales Manager at the Publisher's address

Library of Congress Cataloging-in-Publication Data

Friedman, Dave.
    Shelby GT40 / Dave Friedman.
        p.   cm.
    Includes Index.
    ISBN 0-7603-0013-5
    1. Ford GT40 automobile--Pictorial works. 2. Automobile racing-Pictorial works. I. Title.
    TL215.F7F75   1995
    796.7'2'0973--dc20   94-43008

On the front cover: Carroll Shelby poses with one of the Ford GT class race cars before leaving Los Angeles for Le Mans, where the Shelby-built Fords achieved the success Ford had so badly sought against the world's finest race competition.

On the frontispiece: During practice for the 1965 Le Mans race, Phil Hill and Carroll Shelby discuss changes made to the cars in the week before the race. Shelby's hand rests on one of the tails that was added for stability.

On the title page: During the Sebring race in 1965, this Ford piloted by the team of Richie Ginther and Phil Hill was competitive until its suspension gave out.

On the back cover: The car of Bruce McLaren and Ken Miles at speed at Le Mans in 1965. Also, during a pit stop at Daytona in 1965, the car driven by Ken Miles and Lloyd Ruby gets a fresh set of brake pucks and some oil.

Printed in Hong Kong

contents

acknowledgments

No one can complete a book project like this without a lot of help from their friends and I had a great deal of help.

Carroll Shelby was my mentor. If he had never hired me to do the job, the photographs in this book would not exist. Carroll added much to this book with his always-colorful insight.

Carroll Smith, who was the team manager for the Shelby American Ford GT program, has been a great help. He has let me access his very complete file of race reports and test records and he let me copy everything that I needed for this book. Herlita Navidad of Carroll Shelby's office has tracked down a lot of race records and other material for me. Ray Geddes, former Ford Special Vehicles Sports Car Manager, went through his vast collection of records and let me have copies of whatever I wanted. Lee Holman has contributed copies of the few remaining Holman & Moody race reports and some very rare color photographs taken by his father, John Holman. There are a great many discrepancies in the magazine and book race reports. All facts regarding strategy, race results, DNFs, and technical changes are from the official Shelby American and Holman & Moody race and test reports and, in some cases, differ from previously published reports.

Good friends Alexis Callier, Steele Therkleson, John Ohlsen, Kathy Ager of LAT, and Shiela at Ford GB helped supplement my photographs. To them, a huge thank you. The color shots of the early GT40 tests, taken by John and Jean Ohlsen, are extremely rare and maybe the only ones that exist. Not only was Steele Therkleson a fine engine builder, he was a damn good photographer who always had his camera behind the scenes. Many of the later color test photos, again

extremely rare, were taken by him. He has also provided some of the color pit photos used in this book.

Many of the former drivers and crew members have taken time to share their experiences and memories with me. Among those are Dan Gurney, A.J. Foyt, Lloyd Ruby, Mario Andretti, Bob Bondurant, Dick Hutcherson, Lee Holman, Bill Eaton, Charlie Agapiou, John Ohlsen, John Collins, and Steele Therkleson. Former Ford engineer Bill Holbrook conducted the crash test on the Mk. II and shared his information with me. Gordon Burns of Ford Motor Company was vital in getting the crash test pictures to accompany Bill Holbrook's interview. Several drivers of the opposition have also given their insight of what it was like to race against the might of the Shelby Fords. Among those drivers are John Surtees, Peter Sutcliffe, Vic Elford, and Jim Hall. Phil Hill and Chris Amon drove both for and against the Fords and offer a very special insight into the period. Peter Sutcliffe and Chris Amon, two of the three surviving Ferrari team drivers from the 1967 Le Mans Race, explain the heretofore unpublished Ferrari strategy for breaking the Fords.

Maggie Logan Moore helped with the darkroom work and photo selection. My special lady, Susan corrected and edited my grammar, sentence structure, and spelling errors.

Mary Benjamin and Steve Lewis allowed me to use Alta Coffee in Newport Beach as a refuge from all of my outside distractions in order to complete this book project. To them, a huge thank you.

All of my quotes are from taped or filmed interviews. Most of the Bruce McLaren quotes come from his legendary column, "From The Cockpit", that appeared in *AutoSport* for many years. I hope I got most of it right.

Susan, if we'd been together during this period of our lives, it would have been one a hell of a ride.

foreword

I first drove for Shelby American in the Daytona Coupe at Le Mans in 1964. I was teamed with German driver Jochen Neerpasch and we led the GT category until we got caught using an illegal battery to jump start our car during a pit stop and were disqualified.

In 1965 and 1966 I drove the Ford GTs for Shelby American. I will always remember my second drive that year, it was at the Nurburgring. I got a great start and was running in a top position when I ran out of fuel two miles from the pit and had to push the car back to the pits. We had a pit signal mix-up and I thought I was to come in on the following lap. At Le Mans, I teamed up with Phil Hill in one of the new long-nosed 427 Mk. IIs. What an experience that was. I had never driven anything like that, the bloody thing was an absolute rocket- ship. If we would have been able to keep the gearboxes together, I'm sure that we would have finished one and two. There was nothing there that year that could stay anywhere near us.

In 1966 the cars were much better prepared, and the whole team was better organized. By the time we got to Le Mans, Bruce and I thought we had a damn good chance to win. Driving there with Bruce was very special. The car was done up in the New Zealand sporting colors of black and silver and the crew had even painted a fern and the initials N.Z. on the side of the car. We won in what was probably the most talked about and controversial finish in the history of that race. It was the biggest win that either Bruce or I had achieved up to that time in our careers and it is something that will always remain very special.

The people that I worked with at Shelby American were really top notch. They were some of the best and most professional people that I was ever associated with during my racing career. They were always ready to listen and make the changes that we suggested and, God, could they party after the race.

Those were some of the most memorable years that I have ever known, and I will treasure them for the rest of my life.

Chris Amon

Co-Le Mans Winner 1966

preface

The period from January 1965 to September 1967 was, in my opinion, one of the greatest eras in the history of sports car racing. The epic duels in the endurance and sprint events pushed sports car racing to a new level and provided the racing world with some of the most thrilling competition ever seen to that time or since.

This book is not about chassis numbers or technical detail. Those books have already been written by people far more qualified than I. The objective of this book is to focus on the seldom- or never-seen photographs from the Shelby American archive. It is also about the people of Shelby American who turned the Ford GT program into a winner after an initial season of humiliating losses. It was the perfect decision for Ford to turn that program over to us because our team knew how to win. This book is also about our competition, which, during those years, was formidable. Fortunately most of the living drivers and crew members of those cars are my friends and have shared many wonderful stories with me. My only regret is that I don't have enough room to use them all. Some of the most fascinating information that I came upon was the information written in the Ford Pre-Race Reports. These were like scouting reports and they revealed that Ford not only feared Ferrari and Chaparral, but respected them. These reports also revealed some of Ford's weak points.

During that period the Shelby American Fords were challenged by a number of legendary competitors. Holman & Moody, Alan Mann, and Ford Advanced Vehicles also fielded strong Ford-backed teams and, at times, these teams were both allies and competitors. The very strong Chevrolet-pow-

Author Dave Friedman at Daytona, 1965
One of the Shelby crew members grabbed one of my cameras at Daytona in 1965 and recorded some crazy bastard sitting on the ground, taking a picture of the Miles/Ruby Ford just as it was ready to leave the pits. You certainly wouldn't get away with this today.

ered Chaparral 2D and 2F provided fans a chance to see advanced technology at its futuristic best. Porsche with its "giant killer" 904s, 906s, 907s, and 910s were always ready to pounce if the larger-displacement cars faltered. Although Porsche didn't have the speed at that time, they did have reliability, and that's what they counted on. The beautiful Lola-Aston Martin appeared at Le Mans in 1967, and, had it not been for some engine problems, might have been a very serious contender. Ferrari, of course, was our principal competition. Although cast in an unfamiliar underdog position, the magnificent 330 P2, 330 P3, and the 330 P4 prototypes provided Shelby with all of the headaches that he could have ever wanted. Using all of their years of racing experience, outstanding drivers, and shrewd team management, Ferrari held their own against the might of the American corporate giant. They also provided an engine sound that thrilled their competitors and fans alike.

I have tried to stay away from discussing any of the politics that went on during that time between Ford and the different Ford teams. Although I saw and heard many things and had some very definite opinions about the way things were being done, I was not privy to any of the "corporate procedure." My job did not dictate following any set procedure. My only job was to get the coverage for Shelby American and as long as I did that, everyone was happy. Any political views expressed in this book are direct quotes from the person being interviewed. I think that Chris Amon summed it up perfectly when he told me recently, "It's amazing how it all came together, given the long chain of command and all of the politics."

1

1964-1965
Building a Winner

On a cold, dark, rainy day in mid-December 1964, the whole face of Shelby American changed forever. It was on this day that a TWA air freighter arrived at Los Angeles International Airport carrying the first of two Ford GT40s that had been turned over to the Shelby team to prepare for the 1965 racing season. I was there along with driver Bob Bondurant to meet the plane and take the first photographs of the cars as they arrived.

It was no surprise to us that we were finally given this program. I think the biggest surprise for all of us was that it didn't happen sooner based on the less-than-successful Ford Advanced Vehicle racing program. Our race shop in Venice, California, was already working to maximum capacity and this new arrival—and the one that followed later in the week—caused additional problems for a already overworked racing department. How this perennial loser (no wins, no finishes) was transformed into a winner in less then eight weeks is another of the great racing stories that helped mold the Shelby American legend.

Almost from the day the GT40s arrived, a continuous test program at Riverside and Willow Springs was instituted and our test drivers Ken Miles and Bob Bondurant were kept very busy. It seemed like one or both of the cars were testing somewhere everyday. Numerous changes to the suspension, brakes, ducting, transmission, and engine were made, and the car's reliability, which had been sadly lacking, was quickly improved. Team Manager Carroll Smith said it best: "We weren't afraid to cut, hack, and experiment. The English were."

Ford's racing plan for 1965 was rather simple. According to a Ford racing directive, the goal was to "build up a high level of performance consistent with the objective of finishing and winning a major race."

Now it was on to Daytona to see if our ideas were the right ones.

1964
24 Hours of Le Mans

Left:
The Ginther/Gregory Ford left little doubt who had the fastest car in the early going at Le Mans. Ginther took the lead on the second lap and pulled away until transmission problems put the car out in the sixth hour. The Berney/Nobler Iso Rivolta (1) trails Ginther.

Above:
Although the Ford GT debuted at the Nurburgring, there was no question that the center of the project's focus was Le Mans. An impressive three-car team was entered for the 24-hour event. Bruce McLaren (in dark sweater) checks out the car that he and Phil Hill will drive in the race while the two other cars sit in the background. Car #11 was driven by Richie Ginther and Masten Gregory, and #12 was driven by Dick Attwood and Jo Schlesser.

1964

Nassau Speed Weeks

At Nassau, both of the Fords suffered from the lack of proper preparation and a lack of interest. Neither of the cars were competitive, and according to the official race records, Bruce McLaren lasted only three of the five laps of the Tourist Trophy preliminary race before going out with suspension failure. This car was parked for the duration of the Nassau event and not run again until it was turned over to Shelby.

Above:
Phil Hill did not fare much better at Nassau. Hill finished third in the five-lap Tourist Trophy preliminary race and lasted only 17 laps in the Tourist Trophy race before retiring due to suspension failure. Neither of these cars started the Governor's Cup Race or any of the remaining Nassau races, contrary to what has been reported in other books.

Right:
A rather disconsolate John Wyer (white shirt on the right of the car) helps to load the Fords as they prepare to be flown back to England prior to being flown on to Los Angeles. The Ford report on the Nassau race said, "Because of the failed objectives, we must accelerate our original plan to transfer the Ford GT racing program to Shelby American."

Two cars were shipped to Shelby via the Nassau Speed Weeks in December 1964. Both cars are seen here in the cargo hold of the ship on the way from Florida to Nassau.

1964

Arrival at Los Angeles

Above:
It was a cold, rainy day in mid-December 1964 when the first of the Ford GT40s arrived at Los Angeles International Airport.

Top:
The second car arrived a few days later completing the transfer from F.A.V. to Shelby American.

1964

Shelby's Venice, California, Shop

Upon arrival at the Venice shop, the cars were given a complete steam cleaning. Mechanic Frank Lance makes an adjustment in the engine compartment while John Ohlsen (at the rear of the car) prepares to clean the back end of the chassis with cleaning solvent under the watchful eyes of curious Shelby employees.

"When we first got those two cars, they were a mess. Those two cars were totally used up. Frank Lance and I had to start to work immediately because we had so much work to do and there wasn't much time to do it before Daytona."—*John Ohlsen*

As soon as the cars arrived, they were stripped and prepared to be taken to Riverside for initial testing. Here we see the F.A.V. radiator and brake ducting that were soon to be discarded and improved. Also the Borrani wire wheels were soon replaced with Halibrand magnesium wheels.

Engines were removed and replaced with Shelby-prepared 289s.

John Ohlsen positions the Shelby engine prior to bolting it into the chassis.

"The first thing we did was pull the F.A.V. engine and put one of ours in there. We also pulled out the dry sump system and installed our wet sump system. That was a reduction of 50 pounds (lb) right there."—*John Ohlsen*

Jack Hoare of the Shelby American engine shop gives the engine of the GT40 one last tweak before leaving the Venice shop for the first testing session at Riverside. This test occurred in late December 1964.

"Jack Hoare was one of the Shelby team's greatest characters, but he was also one of the best engine builders that I ever saw."—*Steele Therkleson*

1964

First Test at Riverside

Right:

When the car arrived at Riverside, test driver Ken Miles set to work testing the suspension before taking to the track. Miles' son Peter stands at the far left of the car with one of his friends while Shelby engine man Jack Hoare stands next to Miles.

Left:

Ken Miles exits Riverside's turn six and heads for turn seven early in the first test session. When I asked Ken what his first impressions of the car were, he replied, "It's bloody awful." The only changes that had been made prior to this test were a coat of paint, a steam cleaning, and a new engine.
New Shelby American GT40 team manager Carroll Smith remembers that Miles absolutely hated the car and didn't even want to drive it until certain suspension modifications were made.

Below:

A large crowd gathers around the Ford GT40 during one of its initial tests at Riverside. Phil Remington (white shirt) talks to Ken Miles (in car). Behind Remington stands John and Jean Ohlsen, and John Morton stands to the left of Remington.

1964

Early Test at Riverside

Top:
Bob Bondurant shared seat time with Ken Miles for all of the GT40 tests prior to Daytona.

"When we first got the GT40s, they didn't handle all that well. We had problems with both understeer and oversteer and the suspension was terrible."—*Bob Bondurant*

Bottom:
Bob Bondurant lets it all hang out coming out of Riverside's turn eight.

"The wire wheels didn't work very well and the narrow tires caused the car to slide around a lot. The Halibrands and the wide Goodyears made a great deal of difference. We lightened the car considerably and changed all of the suspension components. When we got done, the cars worked really good."—*Bob Bondurant*

Bob Bondurant (far left) watches John Ohlsen and Jack Hoare make some changes prior to returning to the track during one of the early Riverside tests.

"John Ohlsen and I worked really well together. He was really great and I loved him working on my car."—*Bob Bondurant*

Left:
Ken Miles and John Ohlsen discuss changes that needed to be made. Bob Bondurant looks unsure.

Left:
Jack Hoare makes some engine adjustments as Phil Remington looks on.

Below:
John Ohlsen makes some minor adjustments at Riverside as Bob Bondurant looks on.

1965

Early Test at Riverside

The modified hood section shows the ducting needed to cool the new larger-capacity radiator and the larger front brakes.

Above Left:
Carroll Smith (left) and Phil Remington hold the modified rear GT40 body section so that it can be photographed. Note how the fenders have been widened to accommodate the wider wheels and tires to be used during the 1965 season.

"When we took over the GT40 program from the English, we weren't afraid to cut and hack and that's how we transformed those cars into winners in eight weeks."—*Carroll Smith*

Left:
John Ohlsen (far left), Phil Remington, Carroll Smith, and two unidentified Shelby mechanics work on the GT40 during the Riverside tests in January 1965. Note the large rear engine oil cooler mounted in front of Remington.

"The one weak point we had with the car was the Colotti gearbox. We replaced the stock gears with special gears made for us by Ford, but that gearbox was chancy at best. If you shifted smooth, you could make it live. By the time we went to Daytona, those two cars were pretty damn good."—*Bob Bondurant*

1965

Fine Tuning at Willow Springs

"Tuft testing" at Willow Springs just prior to leaving for Daytona. Carroll Smith (red sweater) tapes yarn tufts on the hood as John Ohlsen (behind Smith) works on the test equipment. The tufts were for aerodynamic testing, and showed which way the air flowed.

John Ohlsen fine tunes some of the test equipment as one of the computers sits in the cockpit of the GT40.

"We also started evaluating the aerodynamics on the car. That was the first time I came across Herb Karsch and his people from Aeronutronics. They installed an onboard computer in the car to evaluate the airflow. That computer was huge by today's comparison."—*John Ohlsen*

Below:
The Shelby modified front end is apparent here. John Ohlsen stands to the right rear of the car. Ken Miles is seated in the cockpit and Phil Remington (light green shirt in group on the left) is barely visible among all of the engineers. This test was conducted at Willow Springs, a god-awful place in the middle of the desert.

Left:
The engine and gear box coolers were moved to the rear of the car as seen in this photograph. The unreliable Colotti gearbox was also highly modified by replacing the stock gears with new gears manufactured by Ford.

"Those Colotti gearboxes had never lasted more than about six hours and they would leak like bloody sieves. We had a guy at Ford who was an Englishman and he designed some new ring and pinion gears for the Colotti. The result was that the damn thing lasted twelve hours at Daytona and won."—*John Ohlsen*

Right:
One of the modified GT40s photographed just before departure to Daytona. The wide Goodyear tires, Halibrand Wheels, and engine and gearbox coolers and ducting are seen here.

"One of the biggest and most important changes we made were the wheels and tires. Those new wheels saved another 30lb. We also changed all of the ducting, oil and transmission coolers, and we installed a larger radiator."—*John Ohlsen*

1965

Race Prep at Daytona

Above:
Notes about changes to be made after practice.

Above:
Carroll Smith consults with Ken Miles during one of the early practice sessions at Daytona. The Halibrand wheels, Goodyear tires, and new ducting in the rear body section are visible here. Cobra coupe drivers Ed Leslie and Allen Grant stand on the wall as Bob Johnson and Jerry Grant converse in the background.

"When we went to Daytona, everyone was worried that we'd start breaking gearboxes again as the cars had done in 1964. I told Carroll and the Ford people that if we shifted smoother and a little slower, the gearboxes would last, and they did. Those were the things that Ken and I learned from having so much test time in the car."—*Bob Bondurant*

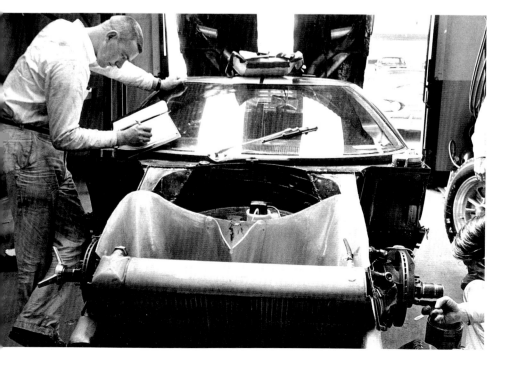

Left:
John Ohlsen makes note of the changes he has made on one of the GT40s at Daytona. Note the larger radiator and improved ducting on the exposed front end of the car.

"Nobody knows how much development went into those cars from the time we got them until they won at Daytona."—*John Ohlsen*

1965

Practice at Daytona

Above:
The Bondurant/Ginther Ford just prior to the start of the race.

"Ken and I really got those two cars really handling well and stopping well during our testing sessions. Richie came up with the idea of front chin spoilers at Daytona. Before we added these, the cars were lifting at speed through the banking and pushing real bad. Once we added these, the problem was cured."—*Bob Bondurant*

Ken Miles leads the Cobra coupe of Allen Grant and Ed Leslie out of the infield and onto the banking during Daytona practice. Changes to the front end were soon to be made.

Right:
Bob Bondurant prepares to go out for practice as John Ohlsen gives last minute instructions. Gordon Chance, Carroll Smith, Phil Remington, and Jack Hoare appear in the background in the white team jackets. Frank Lance wears Lloyd Ruby's red jacket.

1965

Shelby American Race Team

Ken Miles, along with Bruce McLaren, developed the GT40 into a winner. Miles' contributions to the entire Shelby program were monumental.

Bob Bondurant did a lot of the initial testing of the Shelby GT40s with Ken Miles. Bob contributed a great deal to the Cobra world championship program in 1964 and 1965.

Carroll Smith, the Shelby American GT40 race team manager from 1965 to the end of the program in mid-1967. Smith ran the Ford GT team as a separate team wholly apart from any other Shelby race cars.

Phil Remington, Shelby American Chief Engineer. There wasn't a job that he couldn't do, and he did them better than most. As fabricators go, he was one the best.

Richie Ginther was one the greatest development drivers in the history of the sport. He only drove the GT40s for us at Daytona and Sebring in 1965.

Lloyd Ruby was one of the top championship car drivers of the era and one of the first oval track drivers to show natural talent at road racing.

"The first time I ever met or drove with Ken Miles was at Daytona in 1965. Ken was a high-strung Englishman and I was a low-strung Texan. Everybody was wonderin' how the hell we got together but it was Carroll Shelby that teamed us up. Once we got runnin' together, I really enjoyed being with him. We both liked the same setup on the car and we were both equal. We won several big races together and Ken was a really good driver. He did a lot of the testing on those cars and that was a big help to me."—*Lloyd Ruby*

1965

Daytona Continental 2000 KM Race

Below:

Bob Bondurant has taken the lead and is pulling away by the time he reaches turn four.

"I got off to a great start at Daytona. We had qualified second to Surtees' Ferrari and because it was a rolling start, I got a big jump on John's car. By the time we got to the back straight, I was pulling away and leaving the others well back. I was flat out through turn four when I realized that the course markers had been set out across the oval signaling that we would make the left turn into the infield. I thought 'Oh shit, I'm never going to stop.' and I didn't. I went through the pylons, stopped and turned around. By the time I was signaled back on the track I was almost last, but we carried on and finished third. I hadn't paid attention very well at the driver's meeting that morning, and I thought we were supposed to do two laps at speed instead of one around the oval. It was one of my most embarrassing moments."—*Bob Bondurant*

Above:

Parade lap before the green flag is given on the 1965 Daytona Continental. John Surtees in the Ferrari 330P2 (77), Bob Bondurant in the Ford GT40 (72), Walt Hansgen in the Ferrari 330P (88), and Ken Miles in a Ford GT40 (73) lead the field.

Bondurant leads Gurney (44), Miles (73), and Surtees (77) through the
infield as he unlaps himself.

"Once we got behind they didn't want us to push too hard because of the
gearbox. Richie and I knew how to save the gearbox so we pushed a little
harder than we were supposed to. We started getting the slow sign so we
slowed when we came around in front of the pits and sped up once we
went around the corner."

—*Bob Bondurant*

The brilliant John Surtees qualifies the new Ferrari 4-litre 330 P2 on the pole for the Daytona Continental 2000 KM (1,243 mile) Race. Surtees qualified at 2.00.6 miles per hour (mph) and the Ford GT of Bondurant/Ginther qualified at 2.01.8mph.

"I thought Rodriguez and I were in a good position to win at Daytona even though we were a bit down of top speed there. I was running with Gurney's Lotus Ford but I had a big scare when a tire burst, at speed, on the banking. We managed to get back to the pits, but we retired later due to suspension failure. The one problem that we had with the P2 was the tires going away on us on the banked circuits at Daytona and Monza. This was caused by the slightly ancient suspension geometry, which worked quite well on normal circuits but failed us on banked circuits where we ran into the tremendous G Forces encountered there. This Ferrari was a very user-friendly car and you could drive it flat out from the first hour to finish, which you couldn't do with the Fords."—*John Surtees*

Top Right:
Ken Miles at 190+ mph on the banked oval of Daytona International Speedway.

Right:
Bob Bondurant leads the Porsche 904 of Kolb and Heftler through the infield.

1965

Pit Stops at Daytona

The Miles/Ruby car is in for a pit stop and driver change. Engine man Jack Hoare stands at the right while Frank Lance (foreground) changes the brake pucks and Gordon Chance (behind Lance) adds oil.

Above:
John Ohlsen (right) changes the brake pucks on the Bondurant/Ginther GT40 while Frank Lance (left) changes the front tire.

Left:
Shelby crewman hold night signaling boards. Who says it doesn't get cold in Florida?

Above:
A rare photograph of the two Shelby GT40s running together in numerical order.
Bondurant leads Miles through the infield at Daytona.

Next page top:
Bob Bondurant leaves the pits after his final pit stop. Note
John Ohlsen's miner's light on his forehead. These lights
provided crewman with additional light in the very dark pits at
night and allowed them to keep both hands free.

Right:
The final night pit stop for the winning Miles/Ruby Ford.

1965

Victory at Daytona

A tired but happy crew waits for its chance at the champagne. Left to right: Roy Lund, Jack Hoare, Charlie Agapiou, Bob Bondurant, Phil Remington, Frank Lance, Jim O'Leary, and Gordon Chance.

Victory at last for the Ford GT40, and the Shelby team did it in its first attempt. Left to right: Ken Miles, Carroll Shelby, Lloyd Ruby, Leo Beebe, and Ray Geddes celebrate the win.
  "Carroll Shelby played a big part in the success of our program. He was a good manager, advisor, strategist, and he was great with people. Most of all, he was a winner."—*Leo Beebe*

1965

Race Prep for Sebring

Above and Right:
When the cars returned to the Venice shop, they were stripped, overhauled, and tested prior to being shipped to Sebring.

Two of the finest test drivers ever, Bruce McLaren and Ken Miles, compare notes in the Shelby trailer. The contributions that these two men made to our program were staggering.

The Miles/McLaren Ford undergoes pre-race preparation in our hangar at Sebring. Carroll Smith discusses team strategy with John Wyer off to the right of the picture.

"This was my first race with the Shelby setup and it was certainly different from most of the other teams that I have come across. As I see it, it's a team of chiefs that work like Indians. The men doing the job have all of the knowledge, experience, intelligence, and enthusiasm you could ever hope for. Mention anything you like and they know what you are talking about. If you want something special to try, they get it set up, and quickly. They have a really good man in Chief Engineer Phil Remington and they even have a couple of New Zealanders, John Ohlsen and Ron Butler, working on the team. Shelby has time to just stand back, do his thinking, and let the crew get on with it."—*Bruce McLaren*

1965
Sebring Racing

Karl Schmidt , Franz Wiez, and Chaparral team manager Roger Penske push the Hall/Sharp car to its starting position.

"The Chaparrals represent serious opposition. They have been in competition in the US for over two years and are developed to a high degree of durability. They have also tested at Sebring and run eight seconds under the lap record. They have also run a 10 hour endurance test with no problems."—*Ford Sebring Pre-Race Report*

Richie Ginther (10) gets his Ford sideways after a fast start as Ken Miles (11) is just getting underway behind the two Chaparrals.

"I managed to persuade Ken that he was better at Le Mans starts than I was, and Richie started the other car. Richie made one of his lightning starts and led the first lap."—*Bruce McLaren*

Bill Eaton signals to Phil Hill about an upcoming pit stop.

Bruce McLaren at the wheel of the prototype-winning GT40.

"It surprised me to see how competitive the GTs felt. It was obvious that the Shelby team had done a great deal of work on the cars. The handling, braking, and acceleration were greatly improved by the bigger tires and wider rims. Some re-ducting around the front end improved both the brake and engine cooling. The Achilles' heel, the gearbox, while still not exactly a delight to use, was at least reliable with a Ford-made ring and pinion."—*Bruce McLaren*

Ken Miles and Bruce McLaren race to a second place overall behind the Jim Hall/Hap Sharp Chaparral. The Ford car won the prototype class.

Dan Gurney at the wheel of the Pacesetter Lotus 19B that he shared with Jerry Grant at Sebring.

"The Gurney sports modified car will race in Shelby colors and use a 289 engine at Sebring. This car will again act as the 'rabbit' as it did at Daytona. Gurney will extend the Chaparrals and the Ferraris and is not expected to finish."—*Ford Sebring Pre-Race Report*

Richie Ginther and his co-driver Phil Hill were having a good run until the suspension tore away from the tub.

"I was working on the Richie Ginther/Phil Hill car at Sebring when the suspension packed up and tore away from the tub early on in the race. It wasn't until much later that I learned that the tub of Phil's car had been burned out in a crash at Le Mans the year before we got it. We were just given the rubbish from F.A.V."
—*John Ohlsen*

Above:
The Ginther/Hill Ford GT40 at speed on the front straightaway during the Sebring 12-hour race.

Frank Lance (left) and Gordon Chance (right) re-fuel the Miles/McLaren car during a mid-day pit stop and driver change while Jack Hoare cleans the windscreen. Fast and efficient pit stops were a Shelby trademark.

The Miles/McLaren Ford GT40 during the early hours of the Sebring race.

The Ginther/Hill Ford GT leads the Tannlund/Wagstaff M.G. through the Webster Turns.

Above:
As dusk approaches, the McLaren/Miles Ford races across the rain-swept Sebring course. "Ken Miles and I certainly appreciated the fact that our car had a roof when the downpour hit. The water was 6 inches deep and flowing in places, and the driving conditions were some of the worst I've ever seen. When the windscreen wiper packed up, we were flying blind and wishing that we were wet and able to see rather than snug and dry and poking along into opaque swimming gloom. I tried to revive the wiper out on course but it was a hopeless maneuver in the pouring rain. I finally pitted and let the crew fix the problem."—*Bruce McLaren*

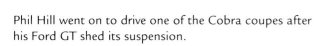

Phil Hill went on to drive one of the Cobra coupes after his Ford GT shed its suspension.

Right:
Frank Lance prepares to signal Bruce McLaren.

1965

Victory at Sebring

The Shelby crew pushes the prototype class-winning car into victory lane at Sebring. This was the second win in as many finishes for the Shelby team's GT40s.

1965

Shelby's First GT40 Roadster

The first Ford GT40 roadster arrived at Shelby American in March of 1965. The car underwent modification and testing prior to being shipped to Le Mans in June.

1965
Testing at LeMans

Above:
The two Shelby GT40s are seen in the pits during the Le Mans test weekend in April 1965. Carroll Smith (cowboy hat) and Bob Bondurant (driving suit) confer with Goodyear tire technicians in the background.

Left:
The #10 Shelby Ford on the track with Bob Bondurant at the wheel. Bondurant set the seventh fastest time of the weekend with a lap of 3:42.9.

Top Left:
Bondurant tested a longer-nose version of the GT40 and reported no significant improvement. The idea was scrapped for the GT40 but appeared on the prototype 427 Mark IIs for the Le Mans race in June.

John Whitmore and Bob Bondurant discuss the roadster that they will share at the Targa in May. This F.A.V. roadster was fitted with a ZF gearbox for the Le Mans test weekend while the Shelby cars were still fitted with their modified Colottis.

Bruce McLaren tests the #11 Shelby Ford during the Le Mans test weekend. "I'm getting quite fond of the Ford GT now. It's a really pleasant car for long distance racing. It's comfortable to drive, quiet inside, and cool inside, which helps reduce driver fatigue."—Bruce McLaren

1965

Racing at Monza and Targa

An interesting fact that has just recently been learned is that the Ford GT roadster raced at the Targa was really a Shelby entry. "The F.A.V. Roadster that was entered at the Targa in 1965 was actually a Shelby American entry that we secured from John Wyer. It was staffed by Shelby personnel and I was the team manager."—*Carroll Smith*

The Miles/McLaren Ford #69 leads a large group of cars on the Monza banking. Miles crashed entering the Curva Parabolica during practice, but the car was repaired. The Amon/Maglioli Ford trails in the fourth-to-last position.

"The full circuit was being used at Monza, which included the banking—which was terribly rough. Although we were instructed by Shelby to 'Go get em,' we decided to save the suspension and maintained a slower pace. As it was, Maglioli had his front suspension break in the fastest part of the banking and he wound up parked next to a Ferrari P2 that had the same problem. We finished third behind two Ferraris, and that wasn't all bad, considering."
—*Bruce McLaren*

Below:

John Whitmore, shown during his four-lap stint in the car he shared with Bob Bondurant. The race was only ten laps long but each lap was 45 miles. The car got up to third overall and could possibly have improved upon that if it had not been for a crash and some other mechanical problems.

"I drove a Ford GT roadster with John Whitmore at the Targa and we had several problems there. During practice we had a continuous oil leak that we thought we had fixed by race time. During the race, the leak returned and by the time I made a pit stop, I had about half an inch of oil on the floor. During John Whitmore's turn at the wheel, the left front wheel came off down near the sea shore. A Sicilian found the knockoff and decided it was his souvenir of the race. Eventually he gave it back to John, and after remounting the wheel, John got back to the pits. I got back in the car and hit some gravel and loose asphalt on the road that hadn't been there the lap before. I lost it and went off the road. I found out that those kilometer markers are really deep in the ground. I hit that thing so fucking hard that it broke the seat belt, shoved the front end in, and put myself up on two wheels. I almost went over but I was lucky enough that I didn't have that much speed, and the car came back down on all four wheels. I walked back to Cerda, found a bar in the hotel, and sat down and had a beer. That's where Carroll Smith found me.
—*Bob Bondurant*

1965
Racing at Nurburging

Below:

At the Nurburgring, the McLaren/Hill GT40 held second place behind the fast-disappearing Ferrari P2 of John Surtees until a half shaft broke seven laps into the race. This was also the only time that a Shelby car ever ran a 325ci engine.

"The Ferraris and Fords were equal in power. Our big disadvantage was that our cars were heavier and that, at the moment, we only have four-speed gearboxes to combat Ferrari's five-speed unit."—*Bruce McLaren*

After the Hill/McLaren Ford broke, these drivers joined in co-driving the Amon/Bucknum car. When Hill took over, he worked the car back up to seventh overall at the end of the race. Hill's vast experience at the Nurburgring paid off.

The chiefs discuss the weekend's proceedings. Left to right, Ray Geddes, Carroll Shelby, Carroll Smith, and Peyton Cramer.

The Amon/Bucknum Ford used the standard 289ci engine. The car ran in the top four until Amon ran out of fuel and had to push the car into the pits. It was concluded after the race that in order to beat the Ferrari 330 P2, the Fords must have 40-50 more horsepower, a fast and reliable five-speed gear box, and a lighter car.

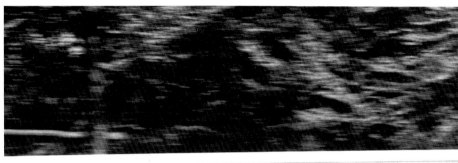

1965
Ready for Le Mans

Right:
Carroll Shelby poses with Ford's Ray Geddes (left) and Leo Beebe (right) before departing for the Le Mans race.

Above:
The Scuderia Filipinetti coupe and the Ford of France roadster await loading at Los Angeles International Airport for departure to Le Mans.

The Rob Walker Le Mans entry departs Los Angeles for Le Mans. The numbers on these cars were not the numbers that appeared on them during the race. These numbers were assigned when the entries were accepted, but were changed later. These three cars were maintained by Shelby American, regardless of the entrant's name.

1965

Le Mans Race Prep

The business end of the Mark II. This engine was estimated to put out approximately 485hp and it was the most powerful engine ever to run at Le Mans up to that time. Most of the original development for this engine was carried out by Holman & Moody in their stock car program.

Left:

The much-anticipated 427 Ford Mark IIs undergo preparation in the Ford garage at Le Mans prior to the initial practice session. "All signs point to the 1965 24 Hour race attracting the fastest cars ever to race on the Le Mans circuit. With the great increase in power in the last 12 months it is more than likely that the Ford and Ferrari prototypes will be capable of achieving 220mph on the Mulsanne straight. The sobering thought is that the men who will drive these projectiles must be carefully chosen, for it is certain that not even a Grand Prix driver has driven anything before which could attain this type of speed."—*AutoSport*

Right:

The very busy and overcrowded Shelby garage. It was just too many cars, not enough people, and too much Ford politics that killed us there. In the foreground, Mike Donovan works on the Rob Walker entry as Carroll Smith (behind Donovan) watches work progress.

1965

Practice at Le Mans

The two Mark IIs in the pit area prior to the start of practice. The cars are seen in their original configuration, which changed considerably by race time. These cars were constructed by Kar Kraft in Dearborn, Michigan, and they were prepared by Shelby American and Ford personnel before shipment to France.

Above:
Bruce McLaren during one of the early practice sessions.

"With seven liters and something like 500 safe horsepower strapped in their tails, the new Fords took a bit of taming. With some chassis tuning and some aerodynamic trimming, these cars were easily the fastest cars on the circuit."—*Bruce McLaren*

In practice, Phil Hill astounded everyone with a remarkable lap of 3.33, or 141.37mph. He also reached 213mph on the Mulsanne and was easily the fastest machine ever seen at Le Mans up to that point.

The Ferrari lineup for the 1965 Le Mans race. The following conclusions were drawn in Shelby race reports prior to Le Mans:

"The Ferrari P2 is more reliable than the GT40, the Ferrari has a great advantage in acceleration, the Ferrari has a slight advantage in top speed, the Ferrari has a great advantage in braking power, and the Ferrari has a great advantage in the speed of shifting, strength of the gear box, and the use of at least five speeds."

Left:
Phil Hill takes time to sign autographs for some of the many fans at Le Mans.

Right:
Pre-race photographs were shot of the modifications done to the tail section to keep the car on the ground at high speed.

Above:
Phil Hill and Carroll Shelby discuss some of the changes made to the big Fords during the week. Note Shelby's hand resting on one of the tails that had been added for stability.

Left:
The Hill/Amon Ford in its final race configuration. Fins and spoilers have been added front and back to gain adhesion and stability at ultra-high speed.

"I made the fins for the Ford Mk. IIs at Le Mans in 1965. The cars had come from Kar Kraft and had never been run. As it turned out we needed, what I called 'Chrysler Fins' to make the cars more stable at high speed. When Roy Lunn explained what he wanted, we went out in the backside, behind the pits, and cut up these large sheets of aluminum and bent them over our trailer. They were a fabricated aluminum piece fitted to the body, which was kind of unique at that time. They were indeed run during the race and worked well. Unfortunately the new Ford gearboxes didn't work as well."—Bill Eaton

"These cars were a bit nervous to begin with when the speeds got around the 200mph mark. With the twin tails, spoilers, and small wings on the front, cruising above the 'double-ton' was safe once you became accustomed to the fact that the Mulsanne had shrunk considerably."—*Bruce McLaren*

63

1965

24 Hours at Le Mans

Left:
A furious and haggard John Ohlsen (white team jacket) trails the Rob Walker entry on its way to its starting position. Bob Bondurant (foreground) steers the car as the three well-dressed pushers observe Ohlsen.

"I remember an incident at Le Mans in 1965 when I was taking care of the Rob Walker-entered GT40, which was actually a Shelby entry. Bondurant and Maglioli were driving for us and the car was running very well. We were well satisfied with everything and thought we had a good chance in the race. The night before the race, we were finishing up with our final race checks when this bloke from Ford shows up with a new engine. I said 'What's that for, our engine is running well, it's strong, and we feel that it will finish.' He said, 'Change the engine, you have nothing to say about it.' We did, and the engine failed three hours into the race. That was the beginning of the end for me."—*John Ohlsen*

Bruce McLaren ran at a record-setting pace until forced out after two hours with transmission trouble.

"During the first two hours, Chris Amon and I enjoyed some real motor racing in the 7-liter Ford GTs. Chris was first away at the start but I cruised by as we pulled on to the Mulsanne straight. We both had to resist the temptation to make those electrifying opening laps a carve-it-up sprint."—*Bruce McLaren*

Bob Bondurant makes a spectacular start.

"I drove the Rob Walker-entered Ford at Le Mans in 1965 and that car worked great. We finally got to where I could go flat out down the Mulsanne Straight by adding some chin spoilers to the front of the car. I was the third-fastest qualifier and got one hell of a start. I got that car up to 212mph on the straight and my balls grew a little bit when I had to brake to 30mph for the hairpin at the end of the straight. I thought to myself, 'Shit, I hope I stay on the road.' They didn't have guardrails in those days, just trees and sand banks. That car worked flawlessly, it was just great. If we could have kept our original engine, we could have done 24 hours easily and possibly won it all as things turned out."—*Bob Bondurant*

Below:
McLaren leads the Peter Sutcliffe/Peter Harper Cobra Daytona coupe through the Mulsanne hairpin.

"This is the first car I've driven that made Le Mans feel like the short circuit at Brands Hatch."—*Bruce McLaren*

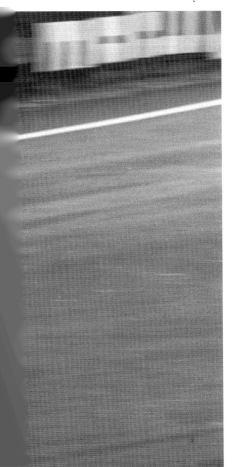

Above:
McLaren and Miles set a lap record of 3:41.2, only to have Phil Hill break it a short time later.

"We learned an important lesson at Le Mans in 1965. We had made the classic mistake of thinking that Le Mans was a speed contest instead of an endurance race. We now realized that it didn't matter how fast you went if you didn't finish. That mistake wouldn't be repeated."—*Leo Beebe*

The Hill/Amon Ford set an official lap record of 3:37.7 (138.3mph) after a 40-minute pit stop to replace a bolt in the transmission. Unfortunately this car retired in the seventh hour with transmission trouble.

"I drove one of the prototype Mk IIs at Le Mans in 1965 with Phil Hill, and that thing was bloody quick. The car was not quite as sorted out as it was in 1966, but, with that long nose, we blew by everything on the Mulsanne straight. I remember that at the start Bruce was in one car and I was in the other. We took off and were running nose to tail and by the time we got around to White House, we could barely see the Ferraris in our rear view mirrors. If the transmissions would have stayed together, we would have walked off with that race. No one could have started to catch us. We absolutely ran off from everyone."—*Chris Amon*

Right:
The Ford of France roadster driven by Trintignant and Ligier was the first Ford to retire. They went out in the second hour with transmission trouble.

The Hill/McLaren Ford, just cruising.

"Gearboxes were the Ford jinx last year, so this year the two big cars were fitted with special four-speed monsters made in the USA. And once again they broke."—*Bruce McLaren*

Right:
The first of the head bolt failures occurred in the Bucknum/Mueller Ford GT40 during the second hour. Several mechanics had warned Ford all year of this potential problem but the warning went unheeded.

"The Ford corporate politics cost us races that we could have won. The race at Le Mans in 1965 was a good example."—*Chris Amon*
"You should have seen all of the finger pointing among the Ford people once things started unraveling. It was almost humorous."—*Bruce McLaren*

1965

The McLaren X1

By September, the McLaren team had developed a lightweight 7-liter roadster for Ford. The plan was to run this car in the North American Professional Series. Chris Amon debuted the car at Mosport in September 1965.

"The X1 car we built at McLaren was bloody hopeless. It was much too far off the pace to be running with the McLarens and the Lolas and It was far too heavy and underpowered."—*Chris Amon*

Above:
Chris Amon approaches turn seven at Riverside. Amon finished a distant fifth, two laps behind the winner Hap Sharp.
By the time the car arrived at Riverside for the Times Grand Prix it had undergone several body modifications to improve the handling and stability. Note the spoiler on the tail and tabs and spoiler under the nose. Bruce McLaren in a McLaren M1B (4) laps Amon (71) during the Riverside race.

"I remember that at Riverside, Ford decided that it was a driver problem, not a car problem, and put a lot of pressure on Bruce to replace me with Johnny Rutherford. I can't remember if Rutherford ever tried to make a lap, but I finally drove the car in the race and I was 5 seconds off the pace. That car was just bloody hopeless."—*Chris Amon*

Right:
Chris Amon's final appearance in the X1 was at Nassau in December 1965. The big car was hopelessly outclassed and failed to finish. This car had been dubbed "Big Ed" by the McLaren crew in honor of Ford's less-than-successful project, the Edsel.

2

1966
A Clean Sweep

For Shelby American, 1966 was a year of great victories and profound tragedy. By January, the Ford Mk. II development and testing program, which had originated in mid-1965, was in full swing and the first race at Daytona was upon us.

Daytona had now become a 24-hour race and anticipation was running high as to the durability of the Mk. II. We knew that we were as prepared as we could possibly be, and, with many of the world's best drivers and mechanics on our team, we could only hope that our racing luck would hold. It did, and we finished all three cars, with Ken Miles and Lloyd Ruby repeating their 1965 overall win. No major problems occurred and the cars were returned to the Shelby American shop in Los Angeles for overhaul.

There were three Ford-sponsored teams competing in 1966. Shelby American would be responsible for most of the car construction and initial testing, and Holman & Moody and Alan Mann Racing would also build cars, field teams, and test. All of the teams operated on an individual basis, but during the races, team orders were adhered to, and those orders came from Ford. Unfortunately, because of the Ford politics, a lot of unnecessary animosity was created between the teams when peace and harmony would have served everyone better.

After Daytona, we turned our thoughts to Sebring and the Le Mans test weekend a week later. Sebring was another success with Ken Miles and Lloyd Ruby scoring a last minute win when the engine blew in the Gurney/Grant Ford. Fords also finished in second and third. While most of the team was at Sebring, John Collins and several others were preparing two Mk. IIs and the J Car for the Le Mans test.

The test at Le Mans was conducted in less than desirable conditions and it resulted in the death of well-known sports car driver Walt Hansgen. Hansgen had not chosen to obey the orders he was given regarding lap times and, while traveling much faster than ordered, he crashed.

Above:
The three Shelby entries were started by three of the world's best drivers. Bruce McLaren (shown here) started the car he shared with Chris Amon. This car was supposed to lap at about 2:08.0, or about 4 seconds off the established pace. This was done to insure that at least one car would finish. If the race went as planned (it did) the intention was to speed this car up to a 2:05.0 to 2:06.0 pace to bring the car up into contention.

"The Ford Mark II had some minor vices and, in comparison to the P3 and P4, was a rather heavy car. It was perfectly suited to Le Mans for which it was really built and it was a very pleasant and comfortable car to drive."—Chris Amon

Above:
Ken Miles, as always, supremely confident before the start of the race. Miles shared this car with veteran USAC driver Lloyd Ruby and they hoped to repeat their 1965 victory. Miles qualified this car on the pole at 1:57.0 and was instructed to lead the race at 2:04.0 to 2:05.0. It was felt that this pace would win the race.

The race at Le Mans was a success with Fords finishing in the top three positions. This race will always be remembered for its controversial dead heat finish. This, of course, didn't go according to plan and it created a controversy that still rages today when we all get together. It was a stupid decision, and it cost Ken Miles a chance to become the first man to win Daytona, Sebring, and Le Mans in the same year.

Although our racing season was over after Le Mans, testing continued. It was during one of these tests that Ken Miles was killed while testing the Can Am version of the J Car. Miles' death was one of the most unbelievable shocks that ever occurred at Shelby American, and it cast a pall over the entire program. It was the most devastating event to happen to us since Dave MacDonald's death at Indianapolis in May 1964. To this day the reason for Miles' crash is listed as unknown, and that's the way it should stay.

Testing continued throughout the rest of the year and one of the most important of these was conducted at Dearborn, Michigan. Shortly after Miles was killed, Bill Holbrook conducted a crash test with one of the early Mk. IIs. Because of this test, a number of significant safety changes were made to the Mk. IIs and were later incorporated in the Mk. IVs for the 1967 season.

Above:
The new Hill/Bonnier Chaparral 2D coupe sits in the pits during practice. Jo Bonnier sits in the cockpit.

In 1966, Dan Gurney, one of the fastest drivers in the world, joined the Ford program. Gurney shared this car with long-time friend and co-driver Jerry Grant and they were instructed to lap at 2:06.0 to 2:07.0. This was done in order to avoid inter-team racing and to keep a car in position to contend for the lead if car #98 dropped out or had problems.

1966

Testing the Mk. II

Jacque Passino (left) and Al Dowd watch a wind tunnel test of the Ford Mk. II early in 1966.

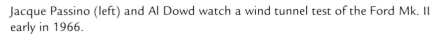

Ken Miles tests gear ratios, chassis settings, engine durability, and brakes at Sebring from January 17 through 24, 1966. Ronnie Bucknum shared the driving chores during this test to establish what it would take to make the Mark II competitive at Sebring in March.

1966
Preparing for Daytona

Right:
Carroll Smith, Phil Remington, and Ken Miles discuss possible car changes during practice.

Left:
The Gurney/Grant Ford practices pit stops during practice week at Daytona. That's crew chief Ron Butler in the white team jacket at the left front of the car.

Race preparation in the Ford garage. The Holman & Moody entry, driven by Walt Hansgen and Mark Donohue, is being given a final check the night before the race. John Holman confers with drivers Donohue and Hansgen in the background. This car finished third overall.

The business end of the Ford Mk. II. Note the metal boxes designed to fulfill the FIA rule for luggage space; not exactly first-class travel.

"Bill Iness had Sully [Don Sullivan of Ford Engine and Foundry] put the 427 engine together to achieve 500hp. They knew that reliability was our most important criteria and they achieved that by running four or five Le Mans races on the dyno."—*Carroll Shelby*

1966

Daytona 24-Hour Race

Bruce McLaren at full speed on the Daytona banking. The Fords reached 196mph on the banking.

"Daytona proved that Ford had solved their engine and transmission problems."
—*Bruce McLaren*

Ken Miles leads Mark Donohue and Bruce McLaren out of the infield onto the high banks during the early part of the race. These three cars ran in this order for a number of laps. The #98 car led the entire race from start to finish, only losing the lead during the first two pit stops.

The third- and fifth-place finishers race together but in reverse order. Bruce McLaren leads Mark Donohue in the Holman & Moody-entered Mk. II. The McLaren/Amon Mk. II had an apparent failure of the limited slip differential roller springs at about the 15-hour mark. This prevented the car from moving up into fourth place as planned.

Right:
Dan Gurney leads Pedro Rodriguez's Ferrari 365 P2 and Jochen Rindt's Ferrari 275 LM out of the Daytona infield. Everything ran to plan and the Gurney/Grant Ford finished second overall.

The Gurney/Grant Ford pits for fuel. Jerry Bondio fuels the car as Colin Riley cleans the windscreen. Behind Bondio, Phil Remington (white jacket) and Bill Eaton watch the action.

The Ford team offers signals from the pits at night.

The only prolonged challenge to the Fords was from the year-old NART-entered Ferrari 330 P2 driven by Mario Andretti (driving) and Pedro Rodriguez. This car finished fourth overall.

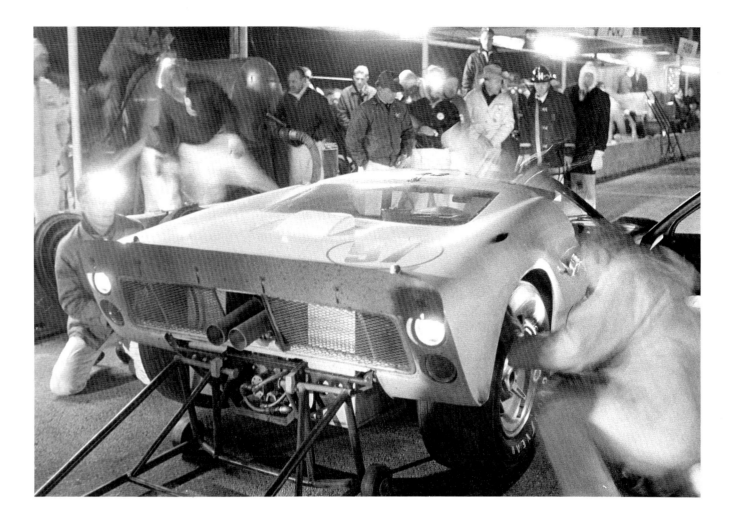

A night pit stop for the Gurney/Grant car. The tired and cold crew is a blur of action as they rush to change tires and refuel. Note the miner's lamps shining brightly on the foreheads of some of the crew members.

The Shelby crew shows the strain of many hours of endurance racing. Phil Remington checks his stopwatches as other crew members try to catch a quick nap.

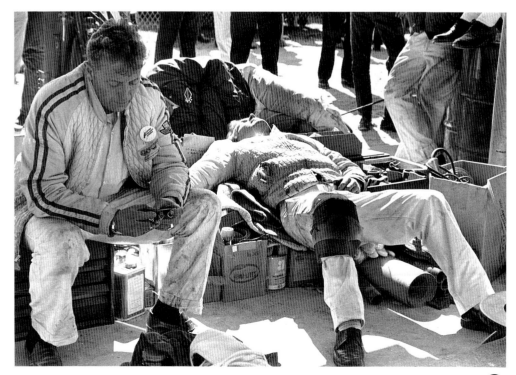

This Ford Mk. II, entered by Holman & Moody, and driven by Ronnie Bucknum and Richie Ginther, was the first Mk. II to compete with an automatic transmission. A two-speed automatic transmission was used and the car finally retired at 4:20 a.m. with a cracked torque converter that caused the loss of all of the transmission oil.

Inset:
Popular driver Ronnie Bucknum was one of the Holman & Moody drivers at Daytona. Bucknum helped debut the Ford Mk. II that was equipped with an automatic transmission.

The well-used winning cars were loaded for transport back to the Shelby shop in California. They did not go directly from Daytona to Sebring. Rather, they went "home" for a rebuild, then came back to Florida for the Sebring race.

Lloyd Ruby (left) and Ken Miles receive the winners' plaudits after winning their second consecutive Daytona Continental. "The Mark II was a really good car. It had lots of power, was fast, and it handled damn good. Ken and I won our second Daytona race with it in 1966."—*Lloyd Ruby*

1966

Race Prep at Sebring

Right:
The Ford hanger at Sebring in 1966. The Shelby cars are undergoing preparation in the foreground while the Alan Mann entries are in the background and the Holman & Moody cars are in the back room at the right.

The crew of the Miles/Ruby roadster pose for a pre-race picture. Left to right: Ron Butler, Eric Leighton, and Colin Riley look confident of their preparation.

Max Kelly, Charlie Agapiou, and Mike Donovan enjoy a light moment before the start of the race.

"At Daytona, Dan Gurney thought that Ken had the better crew, so at Sebring, we switched crews. As fate would have it, Ken won anyway."
—Charlie Agapiou

Right:
Dan Gurney and Jerry Grant discuss car changes with one of their mechanics, who is barely visible through the back window.

Left:
Steele Therkleson, Phil Remington, and Ken Miles change the transmission on the X1 roadster. This car went through two automatic transmissions early in practice and was finally switched to a manual transmission for the rest of the practice sessions, qualifying, and the race.

1966

Racing at Sebring

Start of the 1966 Sebring race. Dan Gurney (foreground) is about to enter his record-setting Ford Mk. II as Mike Parkes, Graham Hill, Walt Hansgen, and Ken Miles rush to enter their cars just behind Gurney. Gurney had set a new qualifying record of 2:54.9.

Top:
The Miles/Ruby Mk. II Roadster was not asked to qualify quickly and therefore this car started in the fifth position. Numerous changes had been made after the car was received by Shelby American from McLaren through Kar Kraft. The chassis was completely rebuilt to SAI specs. The chassis structure was strengthened at the rear hoop joint, crash damage was repaired, a roll over bar was fabricated and installed, and the short nose and substructure were mounted. A coupe tail was fitted in order to utilize proven oil cooler, rear brake, and carburetor air ducting.

Bottom:
The Parkes/Bondurant Ferrari 330 P3 posed a very real threat to the Ford quest for victory. This was the debut race for this car and, although it was a bit underpowered, the car proved that it could lap close to the Ford lap times.

> "It's very difficult coming here with one car and we'll have to play it by ear. I've done a bit of calculation and I think it will take consistent laps at 3:03.0 to win the race, and that's what we will do. The car is superb in its handling and preparation, and we have the reliability to finish."—*Mike Parkes*

The Ferrari ran in the first three for most of the race and retired from the race in the 12th hour with transmission trouble. Parkes' calculations of 3:03.0 were 3 to 4 seconds slower than what the Fords were ordered to run.

Left:
Left:
The two Chaparral 2D coupes offered another potential challenge to the Fords. This challenge failed to materialize with both Chaparrals retiring before the 3-hour mark.

The Gurney/Grant Ford was ordered to lead the race at lap times of 2:59.0-3:00.0 in order to extend the Chaparrals and the Ferraris. This car only surrendered the lead during pit stops until the final minutes when the engine blew on the last lap.

Homer Perry converses with John Holman as Shelby American engine man Steele Therkleson watches the pit action.

"If you had to give the credit to one man at Ford for pulling it altogether, it would have to be Homer Perry. He worked with us very well, he was a good common sense guy, and he kept the politics under control."—Carroll Shelby

Above:
The Miles/Ruby Ford Roadster was instructed to lap at 3:01.0 and to stay within striking distance of the leaders. This car was never lower than third in the standings and ran with the Ferrari, alternating for second and third position, for most of the race.

"Ken felt that, in spite of Dan's outstanding performance, that his car would not finish. He told me that Dan's car was pulling him out of the corners despite the fact that Dan's car was heavier than the roadster. Ken felt that this indicated punishment of the engine."—Charlie Agapiou

Right:
The crew of Alan Mann Racing services one of their two Ford entries. Both of the Mann cars retired from the race in the ninth hour. Alan Mann confers with driver Graham Hill in the background.

Left:
The Holman & Moody Ford entry of Foyt and Bucknum sits in the pits, undergoing service. This car had several lengthy pit stops due to brake problems.

Above:
Jerry Grant is hard on the gas during the afternoon hours of the Sebring race. Grant laps the Ferrari GTO of Slottag/Perkins at this point of the race.

The Foyt/Bucknum Ford Mk. II was equipped with the automatic transmission and finished 12th overall after a number of mechanical problems.

The Hansgen/Donohue Ford Mk. II races through the Sebring darkness on its way to a third place finish. This Holman & Moody entry also suffered brake problems during this race.

Left:
The Miles/Ruby Ford Roadster makes its final pit stop. Ken Miles takes over from Lloyd Ruby.

The Gurney/Grant Ford makes its last pit stop while leading the race. The car is receiving fuel and oil and the scoreboard at the top of the picture indicates the position of the car at this time. Carroll Shelby confers with Dan Gurney and Jerry Grant in the background.

Below:
Leading the race, in the final corner before the finish line, Dan Gurney's engine blew, and he pushed his car to the finish line.

"The damn thing just quit. I guess I must have pushed that car for the final quarter-mile. It's got to get better for us."
—*Dan Gurney*

Carroll Shelby and Dan Gurney discuss the closing aspects of the race.

Al Dowd (left) and Ron Butler, chief mechanic of the winning car, hold the trophy given to the chief mechanic of the overall winning car at the Sebring race.

Ken Miles and Lloyd Ruby celebrate their unexpected victory.

"The car was fantastic. It's a great day for Ford but I'm ashamed to win this way. I'm sorry for Dan. He deserved to win, he was magnificent."—*Ken Miles*

"We drove the Mk. II roadster at Sebring and really lucked into the win there. I was in the shower when I found out I had to go to victory lane. What a shock that was. I guess you never know what's going to happen in the final laps. Gurney and them guys was supposed to win that race and they should have. We were really lucky there."—*Lloyd Ruby*

1966

Testing The New J Car

The J Car at speed early in the test weekend. McLaren and Amon had indicated that the car was squirrelly at 200mph and a spoiler was added to stabilize the car.

"Everyone hated the J-Car except Chris; he loved it for some reason."
—*Carroll Smith*

"I loved the J car that Bruce and I ran at the Le Mans practice weekend in 1966."—*Chris Amon*

Right:
Somebody's idea of a practical joke. Note the Ferrari decal under the number one. It could have been that way had the deal between Ferrari and Ford been finalized. The Ford brass didn't see the humor in this.

This was the instrumentation installed on the second Mk. II and the Ford J Car at the Le Mans test in April 1966. This instrumentation was to record brake, suspension, and engine data in both cars. The other Mk. II was to run a durability test.

Left and bottom:
The J Car after the spoiler, made by Bill Eaton, was affixed to the car by John Collins.

"I built the spoiler for the J Car at Le Mans and John Collins and I installed it. A big part of the success of that team was that we built what we needed where we needed it. That's not true in today's racing. If we needed it in the garage, we built it in the garage. If we needed it at the race, we built it at the race. Those days are gone forever. I was very lucky to work with some brilliant people at Shelby's. There wasn't anything we couldn't do, and well."
—*Bill Eaton*

1966

Tragedy in Testing at Le Mans

The Mk. II, driven for this test by Miles and Bianchi, is being readied for a test run at Le Mans. The instrumentation is barely visible on the front seat of the car. Behind the front fender of the car, Jerry Bondio, Garry Kioke, John Collins, Lucien Bianchi, and Phil Remington perform various chores.

Left:
Lucien Bianchi is at the wheel of the test car as Jerry Bondio and Carroll Smith confer with the driver and Sherman Falconer stands by the rear end.

Bottom:
The Miles/Bianchi test car at speed during the Le Mans test weekend.

Next page top:
The Ford J Car, with its new spoiler, undergoes changes before returning to the test track at Le Mans. Al Dowd (foreground) and Ron Butler fasten down the rear deck lid. Colin Riley stands next to Dowd while Bruce McLaren and Lucien Bianchi converse with writer Denis Jenkinson in the background. In the far righthand center of the photograph, Carroll Smith confers with John Wyer.

Right:
Walt Hansgen prepares to commence the Ford endurance test in drizzling rain.
After four laps of warm-up and initial shakedown, Hansgen brought it in to have
some adjustments made and Hansgen indicated that he was very pleased with the
car's handling characteristics. Hansgen (at left in helmet) waits to return to the
track. Al Dowd (left) and Carroll Smith (next to Dowd) stand in front of Hansgen.

Above:

On lap 11, Hansgen was brought in and told to slow down and lap no faster than 3:50.0 by John Cowley of Ford (right), Homer Perry (not pictured), and Carroll Smith (left). After another five laps, Hansgen was down to 3:49.5 and was brought in again on lap 16. Carroll Smith, again, told Hansgen to slow down and hold a pace at over 3:50.0. By lap 20, Hansgen was lapping at 3:46.8.

Above Right:

On lap 21, Hansgen was observed fishtailing before the Dunlop turn. He apparently tried to enter the escape road where he hit a sand bank on the right side, skidded along the left bank of the road, flipped end over end, and suffered injuries that proved fatal. The estimated speed of the car was 100 to 130mph.

Right:

Carroll Smith (at right with hand up) and Homer Perry (white jacket, behind Smith) survey the crash scene.

"When Walt went by the pits, he went by far too fast to get under the Dunlop Bridge. Chris Amon and I looked at each other and Chris said words to the effect, 'Christ, I hope he can sort this one out.' He didn't, of course, and it cost him his life. I was already running toward the accident scene. Walt was speed-happy that day and he killed himself. I was watching the car for obvious reasons but I guess Chris was watching because Walt was going way too fast for the conditions."—*Carroll Smith*

1966

Race Prep and Practice for Le Mans

Ken Miles and Carroll Shelby pose in front of the Mk. II at Le Mans and most of the Shelby American crew stand behind. Left to right: Bill Eaton, Sherman Falconer, Charlie Agapiou, Carroll Smith, Ron Butler, Jerry Bondio, Garry Kioke, Al Dowd, and Phil Remington.

Five new Mk. IIs were under construction at Shelby American for Le Mans.

Left:
The Shelby crew was joined by crews from Holman & Moody and Alan Mann in order to complete all of the work on the new Mk. IIs by May 22. Bill Eaton and Phil Remington (right) discuss the cars' progress with other team members.

Right:
The three Shelby entries line up for inspection. Ken Miles (shirtless) appears at the front of the red car to be driven by Dan Gurney and Jerry Grant.

Left:
Roger Bailey of Alan Mann Racing installs a 427 engine in one of the chassis at Shelby American.

Bottom:
The lineup of Mk. II Le Mans entries prior to departure from Shelby American in June 1966.

Above:
The McLaren/Amon Ford goes through technical inspection. Max Kelly and Garry Koike are seen to the left of the car and Eric Leighton is seen to the right.

Left:
John Collins (right) and Charlie Agapiou (seated in car) check the car out before practice.

Two of the Shelby entries stand in the pit area prior to going out for practice. The press interest in the Ford entries is obvious. Charlie Agapiou is seen in the lower left of the picture.

Left:
The Peugeot Garage in Le Mans was home to the Ford team in 1966. Mark Donohue (bottom right) inspects the work being done on the car that he will share with Paul Hawkins.

"When Chris and I first saw our car in the garage, we both immediately agreed that we'd never seen a better prepared car."—*Bruce McLaren*

Ferrari wasn't sitting on its laurels either. These cars, although down on horsepower, were still serious threats to the Ford challenge.

Below:
Shelby American mechanic Sherman Falconer organizes the box of brake pucks in the back of the pits.

Shelby American engine men Jack Russell and Steele Therkelson are rebuilding the Ford carburetors.

1966

Le Mans: Gurney Holds the Early Lead

Below:

The start is close and a small portion of the record crowd can be seen in the pits. Gurney's #3 car has taken the pole with a track record of 3:30.4, or 142.979mph. Ken Miles (black helmet) can be seen talking to two drivers in front of the powder blue car. Graham Hill commented at the time, "There were people, people everywhere. It was bloody impressive."

Graham Hill's Alan Mann-entered Ford Mk. II got off to a fantastic start. An impressive field gets away behind Hill.

"I was very quick off the start and pulled out to a tremendous lead. I played it very cautiously on the first lap and braked early at the end of the Mulsanne straight."—*Graham Hill*

Above:
Dan Gurney took the lead from Graham Hill on the second lap and lead for most of the early hours of the race.

"I didn't get the best start, but I took the lead on the second lap and Jerry Grant and I never let up. We lead most of the race, at record speed, until we retired with an overheating engine at the end of the 17th hour."—*Dan Gurney*

Bottom:
Denis Hulme at the wheel of the Ford he shared with Ken Miles. This car was ordered to run laps of 3:40.0–3:42.0, stay behind the Gurney car, conserve its brakes, and use a maximum of 6200rpm to conserve the engine.

"I spent the last few hours of the race trying to work out what could happen to the car. I was also hoping and praying that nothing would happen."—Denis Hulme
"We'll run at the front of the race and keep the Ferraris behind us. We'll let them catch us if they can or we will make them break."—*Ken Miles*

The Bucknum/Hutcherson Ford moves from ninth starting position to third position at the end of the first hour.

"That race track was kind of neat. In 1966 there wasn't no guard rails or nothin', just trees—which people used to hit rather regularly—linin' the race track. When it started raining, I told John Holman that if he wanted that sucker to go any faster he better put someone else in there because I was slowin' my ass down. He said, 'Just keep it on the road, Hutch.' Ken Miles and them guys drove faster in the rain than they did in the dry, but I'd never driven a race in the rain. There were times when I was runnin' down the Mulsanne, in the rain, at night, at over 200mph, where I thought, 'What the fuck am I doing here?'"—*Dick Hutcherson*

The Chaparral 2D of Bonnier/Hill outdistances the Ferrari 275 GTB of Noblet/Dubois (57) and the ASA of Dini/Giunti (61) during the first hour of the race. The Chaparral never posed any threat to the Fords or the Ferraris during the eight hours that it ran. The Chaparral retired with a dead battery after climbing as high as seventh place.

"You couldn't discount the lone Chaparral and the wealth of experience of its drivers Phil Hill and Jo Bonnier."—*Ken Miles*

Above:
The McLaren/Amon Ford motors on during the early going.

"Chris and I enjoyed all of this. Two New Zealanders in a car painted black and silver, New Zealand's sporting colors, what could be better?"—*Bruce McLaren*

Left:
The Holman & Moody entry of Ronnie Bucknum and Dick Hutcherson finished third overall.

1966

Le Mans Carving the Mulsanne Turn

Below:

Dan Gurney leads Ken Miles out of the Mulsanne hairpin. Gurney was told to lap at a pace consistent with both finishing the race and breaking the Ferraris. Gurney was also told to lap at 3:37.0–3:38.0, save the engine, save the brakes, and lead the race.

"There was some talk in the pits that Ford thought that Ken did not follow team orders and pushed Gurney to the point of breaking. That was absolute bullshit. Ken followed his directions to the letter. When he pitted on lap one to fix the door, Ken lost several places. After returning to the race, he had to go like hell in order to get back in second place behind Gurney. That's where he was told to be."—*Charlie Agapiou*

Above:

Bruce McLaren takes the Ford that he shared with fellow New Zealander Chris Amon through the Mulsanne hairpin.

Mario Andretti accelerates out of the Mulsanne hairpin in the Holman & Moody Ford Mk. II. The Andretti/Bianchi started 12th and ran as high as sixth before retiring in the eighth hour with a blown engine.

Ken Miles takes his Ford through the Mulsanne Hairpin.

"I took my time at the start and did up my belts, something the faster starters failed to do. I was away with the Chaparrals and tried to stay out of harm's way. Driving into the late afternoon or early morning sun is a bloody nuisance; you can't see anything, it absolutely blinds you."—*Ken Miles*

1966

Le Mans: Porsche, Ferrari Offer Challenges

Between driving stints, Dan Gurney relaxes by reading the latest Le Mans news. Teddy Mayer watches from behind.

The Shelby crew was very efficient at pit stops and we picked up valuable time during the race because of this. Shelby crewman Ron Butler checks the left front tire while Jerry Bondio refuels the Gurney/Grant car. Goodyear tire technicians check the rear tires.

Top Left:
The view most often seen by the opposition of the
Gurney/Grant Ford Mk. II at Le Mans.

Previous page bottom:

By 1966, Porsche was getting very serious about capturing the overall prize at Le Mans. The fuel-injected 906 Carreras finished in fourth through seventh place behind the three Fords. Although considerably smaller in engine displacement, the reliability of these cars could not be overlooked in the overall picture. The fifth place-finishing Porsche 906 of Schutz and de Klerk leads the 906 of Gregg and Axelsson out of the Mulsanne Hairpin.

Above:

The beautiful Ferrari 330 P3 prepares to accelerate out of the Mulsanne Hairpin with Richie Ginther at the wheel. This Ferrari ran in the top four and even led the race for a bit before retiring with gearbox problems. None of the P3s finished.

"You could never discount the Ferraris. They were down on power, but they were much deeper in racing experience then we were and the talent of their drivers was superb."—Ken Miles

1966

Le Mans: Miles Takes the Lead

Above:

A good illustration of what drivers feared most at Le Mans. The Miles/Hulme Ford passes the Jansson/Toivonen Alpine on the right side of the road. Smaller cars that were 100mph slower were supposed to stay to the right side of the road so that the big boys could pass on the left. Obviously it didn't always work that way and these kind of encounters caused many serious accidents.

> "The landscape goes by very quickly at Le Mans and the biggest problem there is overtaking the slower cars that are 100 miles an hour slower than you are."
> —Ken Miles

Left:

Bill Eaton and Steele Therkleson push the Gurney/Grant Ford to the dead car park after it retired with terminal overheating.

> "We lead them all, set records, and can't finish. Our luck has got to change."
> —Dan Gurney

Right:
Well-known stock car driver Dick Hutcherson prepares to enter the Holman & Moody entry that he shared with Ronnie Bucknum (lower left of photo).

"I got the ride in the Ford GT when Ford pulled out of NASCAR for a while in 1966. Ford and John Holman hired me and Marvin Panch to test these cars at Kingman, Arizona, Riverside, California, and Danville, Virginia. We tested brakes, tires, and just about everything else for durability on a road course, although Kingman was a big oval. After we completed the tests, Ford wanted to know if we wanted to go to Le Mans. We knew that it was a prestige race but it didn't pay any money, so we said no. I told them that I could stay home and make more money running the half-mile dirt tracks than I could by going over there and running at Le Mans. When A.J. got burnt in Milwaukee that year, they called me at the last moment and asked what it would take for me to reconsider. I gave them a certain figure and they told me to get on a certain flight that went through Washington D.C. When we got to Washington, some guy comes to the plane and hands me my passport. I guess they pulled some pretty heavy strings. By the time I got to Le Mans, practice had already started. I never did get very many laps on the race track before the race started, but I could draw the track, as it was then, for you right now."—*Dick Hutcherson*

Left:
Dusk at Le Mans, as it used to be.

Above:
Ken Miles and long-time friend and mechanic Charlie Agapiou confer during a late race pit stop.

"Ford didn't want Ken to win at Le Mans. They wanted the headlines to read 'Ford Wins Le Mans,' not 'Miles Becomes the First to Sweep Daytona, Sebring, and Le Mans.' Ken told me that, in spite of any Ford decision, he wasn't going to finish second."—*Charlie Agapiou*

Above:
Charlie Agapiou (right) changes one front tire while Ron Butler changes the other. Jerry Bondio talks to Shelby as Mike Donovan watches the pit stop from the rear. Note the French officials sealing the fuel tank.

"It was most amusing to see how the pit officials were so deliberate in sealing the caps of the Fords. It was almost comical."—*Denny Hulme*

1966

Bruce McLaren confers with the McLaren team manager Teddy Mayer during the final pit stop.

Le Mans the Famous Blanket Finsih

Below:

The final stop for the Miles/Hulme Ford finds Carroll Shelby telling Miles and Hulme of the decision to have a blanket finish at the end.

"I could tell that something was up regarding the finish but I wasn't advised of what that decision was. We all wanted Ken to win Le Mans after his successes at Daytona and Sebring because he would have been the first to win all three of those races in one year. I don't know what they told Ken during that final pit stop, but he wasn't very happy as he entered the car to finish the race. I leaned over and told him, 'I don't know what they told you, but you won't be fired for winning Le Mans.' He would never talk about it after the race was over and we were the best of friends."—*Carroll Smith*

"After Carroll talked to Ken during the final pit stop, I heard Ken say, in a loud voice, 'So ends my contribution to this bloody motor race,' and he threw his sunglasses across the pit."—*John Collins*

Right:

It had been a long and bumpy road since 1964 but now Ford's racing boss Leo Beebe could be confident of victory.

"I was director of marketing for Ford in Europe when Lee Iacocca called in April 1964 and asked if I wanted to head up Ford's racing program. I told him that I'd never even seen a motor race. He said that was all right, it was an organizational job." [Beebe learned a lot, fast, about racing cars. He also was capable of making courageous decisions. At Le Mans in 1966, he threatened to withdraw the entire Ford team due to a stupid French decision regarding the disqualification of Dick Thompson and his Alan Mann-entered Mk. II. His bluff worked and the entry was restored.] "I was scared to death that they would call my bluff because I didn't have Ford's approval to make such a decision. When Henry Ford saw me at the starting line before the race, he handed me a card that said, 'You better win, HF II.'"—*Leo Beebe*

Right:
McLaren prepares to leave the pits after the last pit stop. Mechanics Charlie Agapiou, Max Kelly, and Phil Remington watch from the pit wall while Leo Beebe (in the top right corner of the photo) points out something to Don Frey.

"I remember when I came in for our last pit stop and Bruce told me that Ford wanted to do a blanket finish. I said, 'Who's supposed to win?' Bruce said, 'I don't know, but I'm not going to lose.'"—*Chris Amon*

Bruce McLaren leads Ken Miles across the finish line in one of the most controversial finishes in the history of Le Mans.

"I wanted Ford to win. We called Ken in and slowed him down so that Bruce and Chris would win. I think that they deserved to win. They ran a good race and did what we had told them to do."—*Leo Beebe*

1966

Le Mans: Controversy in Victory

A furious
Ken Miles is besieged by
spectators seeking autographs, press and
photographers wanting to know what happened.

"In 1966, Ford didn't cost Ken the race at Le Mans, I did, and I regret it to this day. They came up to me and said, 'Who do you think should win the race?' I thought, 'well, hell, Ken's been leading for all of these hours, he should win the race.' I looked at Leo Beebe and said, 'What do you think ought to happen Leo?' He said, 'I don't know, I'd kind of like to see all three of them cross the finish line together.' Leo Beebe did not tell me what to say or do, so I said, 'Oh, hell, let's do it that way then,' not knowing that the French would interpret the rules the way that they did. Ken should have won the race, and in most everyone's mind, he did win the race. That was my fuck-up, I take full responsibility for it, and I'm very sorry for it because, as you know, Ken was killed at Riverside two months later. Every time you go racing, you put your reputation on the line."
—Carroll Shelby

"I knew the ramifications of a dead heat at Le Mans. My job was to know all of those things, but I wasn't consulted when the decision was being discussed."*—Carroll Smith*

Bruce McLaren, Henry Ford, and Chris Amon celebrate the victory at Le Mans.
"After Daytona I said that the Fords could and should win at Le Mans. No one in England would believe me. They said Le Mans is different, Le Mans is a car breaker, you can't beat Ferrari, and now it's all history. This is by far the biggest race that I've ever won and the same goes for Chris. The whole thing seemed to be so simple."*—Bruce McLaren*

1966

A Tragic Ending at Riverside

Right:
Maybe the only photograph of the engine–automatic transmission combination that was being tested by Ken Miles the day of his fatal crash at Riverside.

Above:
The date is August 17, 1966, and it is a day that will end in disaster for the Shelby crew working on the J Car testing session at Riverside. Steele Therkleson (white shirt) works on the Weber-carbuerated 427 engine in the much-modified J Car chassis. The car had been modified to determine its suitability for modified sports car competition.

Steele Therkleson contends that this is the last picture ever taken of Ken Miles alive. The picture was taken about five minutes before he went out for his final laps.

"Everybody has their own version of what happened there, but I don't believe that there was ever a concrete finding. That car was run very hard during the three days of testing and Ken had driven it exceptionally hard. We were going to change the tail section on the car. I'd been dispatched back to L.A. to pick up a new tail and I had arrived back at Riverside earlier than expected. We never had time to put that tail on because we just ran out of time. The accident happened on the last lap, of the last run, of the last day of testing."—Bill Eaton

"At the beginning of the braking area for turn 9, the vehicle went out of control, left the road to the right at about the 250 marker, and dropped approximately 10 feet into the infield. The vehicle flipped, apparently landed on its left rear wheel, broke up on impact, and burst into flames. The chassis unit broke in two and the driver was thrown clear of the major portion of the vehicle. Death was instantaneous. Cause of the accident has not been determined."—Shelby American Test Report

Bottom and next two pages:
"I was the one who conducted the crash test on the Ford Mark II. This was done shortly after Ken Miles was killed. It was after that accident that we got on a real safety kick regarding our race cars. We wanted to hit the wall at 60mph during the test, but we were hampered by all of the cords and cables. At that time we had to tow the car because we didn't have remote control. As it was, we hit at 51mph, which was, I think, the fastest crash test that we had ever done at that time. I wish we'd had today's technology. Then we would have had no problem achieving the speed that we had originally wanted. After that test, we found that when the rocker panels were crushed the pressure would go right up the filler neck and blow the fuel lid off. With the front end crushed, it directed the fuel up and over the entire vehicle and caused a serious fire problem. We used Stoddard Solvent to duplicate fuel in this test because its weight closely matches gasoline. Because of this test, a lot of changes were made. The biggest ones were the addition of fuel cell bladders to prevent fire and a stronger roll cage. One thing we always wanted to do, but never did because they were too large at the time, was add an onboard fire extinguishing system. We did, however, get a extinguishing system in the Mk. IV at Le Mans in 1967, but it was very awkward. We also did a lot of work on the safety belts. We found that a lot of the attaching hardware that was made out of cold rolled steel broke and bent under stress so I made stainless steel fittings. We also added crotch straps and foam backing on the belts. I don't know what happened to what was left of the chassis. I can tell you that it was history, it was completely crushed. We really learned a lot from all of that testing."—Bill Holbrook

1966

Disappointing December Testing

Above:
Ron Butler's sign says it all after the J Car suffered a chassis failure during the December Daytona test.

Left:
A.J. Foyt tests the new lightweight model of the Mk. II at Daytona just before Christmas 1966. The purpose of this test was to establish the durability of the car for the upcoming Daytona race. The test concluded that in order to be competitive with the Ferrari 330 P4, a significant increase in horsepower was needed.

③

1967
The Mk. IV, P4, and Chaparral

Our 1967 season began with a disaster at Daytona. Not only were the cars totally outclassed by the new Ferrari 330 P4, of which a full team was present, but the transmissions wouldn't stay together because of a heat treating problem with the output shaft. Finally, when we ran out of parts, five of the six entries were withdrawn. It had gotten to the point that you could tell time by when the next gearbox was going to break. This was not the way that we expected to start the season.

Sebring saw the debut of the new Mk. IV, and it proved a smashing success. This car broke all the records and won a convincing victory. The only other factory entry, a Holman & Moody Mk. II, finished second in spite of being parked in the pits with a blown engine. Although Ferrari didn't show, Chaparral and Porsche provide plenty of competition. Bruce McLaren and Mario Andretti had the honor of winning the Mk. IV's debut race. It was also Andretti's first big sports car win. Everyone felt that we were ready for Le Mans.

There was no lull between Sebring and Le Mans. Testing continued on a regular schedule at Daytona, Kingman, and Riverside. The team also attended the Le Mans test weekend. By May, the cars for Le Mans had been completed, painted, and fully tested. It was like a dream come true for most of the crew to show up to such a major event totally prepared. It wasn't often that they had that luxury.

Le Mans in 1967 afforded the record crowd (over 300,000) who attended a chance to see the most incredible display of horsepower, noise, driving skill, and suspense ever seen there to that time. All of the great teams were there, in droves. There were twelve Fords, ten Ferraris, six Porsches, two Lola Aston Martins, and two Chaparrals, and they all had their eyes on the big overall prize. This race did not disappoint the fans, who again, turned out in record numbers.

Above:
One of the Chaparral mechanics uses a giant torque wrench to tighten the wheels of the brand new 2F. Bruce Jennings sits in the car while listed drivers Phil Hill and Mike Spence sit on the wall at the left. This car was powered by an aluminum 427 Chevrolet engine and qualified second fastest at 1:55.36 or 118.897mph. Hill and Spence led the race for eighty-eight laps, at a record pace, until Hill crashed into the wall coming out of the infield.

The red Ford of Dan Gurney and A.J. Foyt was the surprise winner. Surprise to everyone but a few of us who actually believed that they could pull it off. Most of the competition, and even the Ford people, had written this car off as a "rabbit" that would lead the race for a few hours and then expire. The script, however, played out differently and the

Above:
Ronnie Bucknum prepares to qualify as Mike Warne confers with Bucknum. Carroll Smith (cowboy hat) is behind Warne and Charlie Agapiou (in white) is coming up at the right. The Bucknum/Gardner car qualified at 1:57.60 or 116.632mph. This was good enough for tenth place.

John Collins and Colin Riley (left) make some last minute adjustments as Phil Remington, A.J. Foyt, and Dan Gurney watch. Gurney qualified at 1:55.10 or 119.165mph to win the pole position.

team voted "Least Likely to Succeed" shattered most of the previous records on their way to a historic all-American win.

After Le Mans, it was all over. The FIA had changed the rules to reduce the engine size to a maximum of 5 liters for the 1968 season. This caused Ford, Ferrari, and Chaparral to withdraw from international sports car racing. With this withdrawal, a very special era of sports car racing vanished into history. The decision was made in an effort to promote safety and to reduce the high speeds that were being achieved on the long European circuits. It is interesting to note that within two years of the rules change, the Porsche 917 was achieving 240mph on the Mulsanne Straight. This was 20mph faster then the 7-liter Fords had ever thought of running.

1967

Gearing up for Daytona

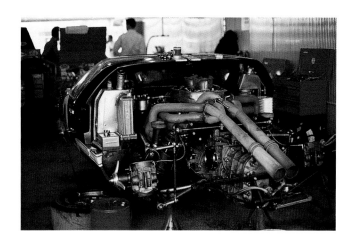

Above:
A Shelby American strategy meeting takes place in the Holman & Moody office. Clockwise from front: Lucien Bianchi (back to camera), Bruce McLaren, Dan Gurney, A.J. Foyt, Frank Gardner, Ronnie Bucknum, and Carroll Smith listen as Al Dowd makes a point.

Above Left:
The business end of the 1967 version of the Ford 427 engine. This version of the 427 featured many modifications including twin four-barrel carburetors. The increased horsepower was a published 500bhp at 6400rpm, up from 486bhp at 6400rpm in 1966.

Left:
Steele Therkleson works on the carburation system on the Gurney/Foyt car.

1967

Daytona: Transmission Troubles Doom Hopes

The Donohue/Revson car lasted 236 laps and retired with a broken output shaft in the gearbox. Note the Mercury name instead of the Ford name on the bottom of the door panel. This was done for this race only.

McLaren and Bianchi began to have problems after fifty-seven laps when they had to pit with overheating caused by ill-fitting body sections. This problem continued to plague the car for the rest of the race.

Chris Amon (Ferrari 330 P4), Dan Gurney (Ford Mk. II), and Pedro Rodriguez (Ferrari P4) ran in this order for many laps.

Charlie Agapiou makes a fashion statement for the well-dressed mechanic at Daytona.

"Several of the Ford people were heard to say that our crew looked scruffy, so I went into town and got a corporate-type haircut and bought a tie. Later on, during one of our transmisson changes, my bloody tie got caught between the gear box and the differential. Bill Eaton took a pair of snips and cut my bloody tie off."—*Charlie Agapiou*

"Charlie Agapiou always gave the appearance of being a character, but he was a really brilliant mechanic, and still is."
—*Bill Eaton*

Below:
Bruce McLaren (left) prepares to enter his car as his crew members finish up their pit chores. This crew combined Shelby American mechanics Max Kelly and Gordon Chance and McLaren Cars employees Tyler Alexander and Gary Knudson.

Left:
The Ford people were kept busy rebuilding broken transmissions.

"We had a little place back in the garage where the Ford people were overhauling the transmissions and we had a line of them ready to go in the cars."—*Bill Eaton*

Right:
The first Ford transmission failure came on lap sixteen and never let up. The poor heat treating of the output shaft was the problem.

"At Daytona in 1967, we got so good at changing transmissions that we were doing it in less then 25 minutes, and that was from car in to car out."—*Bill Eaton*

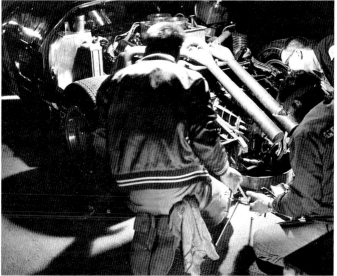

Above:
The Andretti/Ginther entry ran up in second position for a while until Andretti threw a tread and had to pit. They, too, suffered from gearbox failure. The Fords were hard pressed to keep pace with the leaders, let alone lead. In fact, they never led a lap of this race.

Above:
The well-worn McLaren/Bianchi Ford was the only finisher of the six Ford entries. The car finished seventh overall.

"The only reason that this car finished was that we pulled the old transmission out of the J Car, which we had with us in the truck do to our testing schedule. That old transmission was the only one that held up."—*John Collins*

Left:
Phil Remington reflects the mood of the times. It was just one of those days.

The beautiful Ferrari 330 P4 of Chris Amon and Lorenzo Bandini went on to win and ruin Ford's 1967 debut.

"The Ferrari P4 was a lovely car, it was what a Ferrari should look like and sound like, and it was so nimble in its handling. At Daytona, we just murdered the Fords on the infield section of the course. 1967 was a fantastic year. The rivalry between Ford, Ferrari, Chaparral, and Porsche was unparalleled and will never be seen again."—Chris Amon

1967

Andretti and McLaren Team up at Sebring

Bottom:
Bruce McLaren takes a few laps in the wet during the first day of practice. "After half a dozen laps and a few changes to spoilers, roll bars, and tire pressures, I was reasonably happy with the car. When Mario arrived he was also pleased with the setup."—*Bruce McLaren*

The Andretti/McLaren Ford Mk. IV prepares to leave Shelby American for Sebring. Bill Eaton, John Collins (in car), Phil Remington, and Gordon Chance tend to last-minute details. This Color combination must have been a favorite since three different Mk. IVs were painted in this same combination. This led to a lot of confusion among outsiders as to which car was which.

Left and below right: The Ford Mk. IV debuted at Sebring on Wednesday March 29, 1967. Bruce McLaren was the only driver that day since co-driver Mario Andretti was in Atlanta qualifying for a stock car race.

A smiling Mario Andretti reflects his approval of the new Ford. This was Andretti's only race appearance for Shelby American. The rest of his races were for Holman & Moody.

"We have a car that should win the race if practice and qualifications are any indication. We will try to lead the race but we won't abuse the car. We will pace ourselves since 12 hours is a long time and you never know what can happen."
—*Mario Andretti*

1967

Sebring: The Mk. IV's Winning Debut

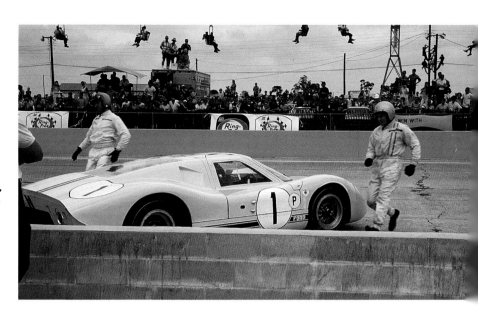

Above:
Bruce McLaren rushes to his car at the start of the Sebring 12-hour race. Mike Spence can also be seen running for his Chaparral 2F. McLaren set a qualifying record of 2:47.6, with the Chaparral qualifying second fastest. This was almost 7 seconds faster than Dan Gurney's record lap in 1966. The Ford drivers were told to lead the race, if possible, at a 2:52–2:53 pace. If the Chaparrals were to lap faster, the drivers were instructed to let them go.

Left:
The two Ford entries run together during the early part of the race. The Andretti/McLaren Mk. IV leads the Holman & Moody Mk. II entry of Foyt/Ruby. This was the way that they finished after 12 hours.

The Spence/Hall Chaparral 2F had trouble getting away at the start and was 30 seconds down by the time they got away. After one hour, Spence had worked his way up to fourth place and by quarter distance, the car was in the lead. During the race between the two Fords and the Chaparral, the lap record was broken no less than twenty times and the Chaparral set the fastest lap of the race at 2:49.0 or 111.032mph. The car finally retired in the eighth hour with transmission problems.

The Johnson/Jennings Chaparral 2D ran as high as fourth place overall before retiring with electrical problems is the ninth hour. This was the final race for the much modified 2D, now sporting a 427 engine.

The Holman & Moody Ford Mk. II, sporting its new body shape, was very quick in the hands of A.J. Foyt and Lloyd Ruby. The car ran in the first three for the entire race and was second for most of it. Half an hour before the finish, the car blew its engine but held on to second place anyway due to the amount of laps it had already covered.

"I think both cars will finish, they're both running very well and we should have no problem finishing one and two."—A.J. Foyt

The Foyt/Ruby Ford and the Hall/Spence Chaparral 2F battle for second place.

Left:
As the crew attends to the Mk. IV on its final pit stop, Carroll Shelby gives the car a lucky pat on the ass. Shelby American Crew Chief Max Kelley summed up the feeling at Sebring. "It's like a lot of 200-mile sprint races interrupted by pit stops."

Right:
The Holman & Moody crew members work on their car as Foyt and Ruby confer on the pit wall. It wasn't long after this that the car was in the pits again with a blown engine.

Above:
McLaren laps the Magwood/Gray MGB on his way to a record-setting performance.

"I'm sorry that the Ferraris aren't here, because on this circuit, with this car, I think we could have avenged Daytona."—*Bruce McLaren*

Carroll Shelby, deep in thought.

Andretti and McLaren accept the spoils of victory. The Ford Mk. IV had scored a major victory in its first outing.

"We had a hell of a battle for a while with the Chaparral and it would have been interesting to see what would have happened if they hadn't had problems. This car is fantastic. I've been involved with the testing of this car from the start, and I think I can say we're ready for Le Mans."—*Mario Andretti*

"We had no problems, and that race with the Chaparral was fun. They were giving us fits and I'm sorry it ended. This car is terrific and everything went as planned. Le Mans in June is going to be an incredible event."—*Bruce McLaren*

1967

Le Mans Practice: Spoilers, and Broken Windshields

Above:
Steele Therkleson works on the engine as Carroll Smith confers with Bruce McLaren, who is sitting in the car. Three different carburation configurations were tried on this car, but none was satisfactory.

Left:
At the Le Mans test days in April, one Mk. IV appeared with Bruce McLaren as the driver. Note the addition of "Chrysler Fins" to the rear deck lid.

Next page top:
The Sebring-winning car tests at Daytona from May 1 to 5, 1967. It was during this test that Al Dowd offered John Collins a crew chief position on a car for Le Mans.

"Al asked me if I wanted a car for Le Mans. This was after Colin Riley quit, and I said yes. He told me the drivers were going to be Foyt and Gurney and I said great, since I'd worked with both of them at Daytona. With those drivers, I knew we could win the race. I said I wanted Mike Donovan and Phil Henney as my crew. Phil was a big help because he could speak French."—*John Collins*

Next page bottom:
Crew Chief John Collins (in white) admires his handiwork at the final shakedown at Riverside just prior to the team's departure for France.

"This was the only time in my racing career that the cars were completely race ready prior to departure. What a luxury."—*Steele Therkleson*

Above:
McLaren at speed with the finned deck lid. McLaren was fifth-fastest of the weekend, but was 11 seconds slower than the Ferrari P4 of Lorenzo Bandini.

"Spoilers and tail fins were experimented with in an attempt to increase high-speed stability. The tail fins provided no increase in stability."—*Shelby Test Report*

Right:
Two of the Shelby cars prepare to go out for practice under the watchful eye of Carroll Shelby (wearing cap). Ron Butler helps his driver get settled in as a group of onlookers gathers.

Some of the Shelby crew takes time for a group picture. From left to right: Steve Scuttack, Phil Henny, Dennis Gragg, Max Kelley, Charlie Agapiou, Gordon Chance, Garry Koike, Dick Wilson, John Collins, and Ron Butler.

Right:
A crisis occurred during practice when the windshields started cracking at high speed in all of the Fords. It was determined that the lamination had been tempered too hard and all of the windshields were replaced with special untempered ones flown in from the States. Gordon Chance, Charlie Agapiou, and Max Kelly replace the windshield in the McLaren/Donohue car.

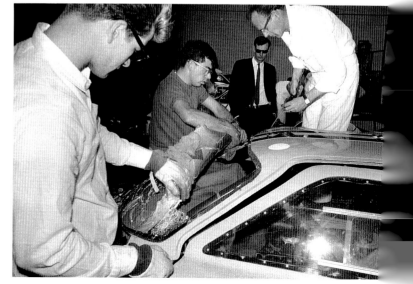

Some of the Fords line up in front of the pits prior to the start of the race. The McLaren/Donohue car is in the foreground. The crew of this car were all dressed in matching yellow uniforms as seen on two of the men working on the Bucknum/Hawkins car in the background.

Bottom left:
Dan Gurney has final adjustments made to his mirror as Phil Remington, Max Kelley, Steele Therkleson, and Charlie Agapiou deal with a problem in the engine compartment.

Bottom:
The 500+ horsepower Ford engine in its final state of racing development for the Ford GT program. Depending on what and whom you read, the published horsepower of this engine varied from 500 to 535hp. Note the finely machined air box.

Above:

The beautiful Lola Aston Martins get a final looking over by the crew.

"That program was a disaster. We wanted to make it a totally British project. Aston voiced an interest in supplying the engines and, in fact, the initial test results were good. We ran for ten hours at Goodwood, and at the Le Mans practice in April we continually put up the fastest times in the wet. In the dry we weren't that far behind Ferrari and Ford. At the Nurburgring we were right in there before we had a suspension failure. We never had a problem with the engine. It was a totally stupid thing that killed the project. Aston didn't keep their feet on the ground and they went and made changes to the engine that we had never tested. The engines that they gave us for Le Mans were never tested. This is something you just don't do, and we lost the head gaskets in the first few laps. It was quite sad because there was no reason why the cars couldn't have put up a very reasonable show when, at that stage, there was no real British involvement at Le Mans. I so much wanted to race against the 7-litre Fords, Chaparrals, and the Ferrari P4s, but it just wasn't to be."—*John Surtees*

Mike Parkes and Ferrari Chief Engineer Mauro Forghieri discuss race strategy just prior to the start.

"I remember talking to Mike during the night and he said that they had set a time to run during the race and were holding to it until the red Ford (Gurney/Foyt) broke. He was convinced that Gurney and Foyt wouldn't last through the night. At about 7 in the morning, with Gurney and Foyt still running, Mike said to us, 'I think we should start to hurry up a bit,' and from then on he and Scarfiotti drove that car absolutely flat out. Parkes and Scarfiotti never quit and they drove that car to the absolute maximum. There is a limit to human endurance and they passed that."—*Chris Amon*

Above:

The magnificent Ferrari 330 P4s prior to the start. The second-place car (21) driven by Parkes and Scarfiotti is in the foreground and the third-place finisher (24) was driven by Mairesse and Beurlys.

"Our primary competition at Le Mans was Ferrari. They had dominated Le Mans for years before Ford finally beat them in 1966 and their experience made up for their lack of horsepower. The P4, Ferrari's primary weapon, was a tremendous machine. It was the best car that the Italian factory had ever thrown into long distance racing."

—Dan Gurney

1967

Le Mans: Gurney and Foyt at a Record Pace

It seems that most of the record crowd of over 300,000 has gathered in the pits for the start of the race. I remember things being so bad that you could hardly move. Ronnie Bucknum in the Ford Mk. IIB (57) got a spectacular start and led the first twenty-three laps at record pace. Gurney (1) is off the line just behind Bucknum as the rest of the field follows.

The Ford Mk. IIB of Bucknum/Hawkins led the first twenty-three laps until they were forced to pit with overheating problems. This car was instructed to maintain a 3:30–3:31 pace but exceeded that during the first few laps. Following Sebring, the IIB was developed as an improvement to the Mk. II. The IIB utilized the same drivetrain as the Mk. IV, was lighter, and featured new nose and tail sections with the air snorkels removed from the rear section. The front brake ducts were relocated and new turbine-styled magnesium wheels were used.

The Gurney/Foyt Ford Mk. IV took the lead after the first hour and never let up. This car was instructed to lap at a 3:30-3:31 pace. If Ferrari or Chaparral were to lap faster, it was decided not to give chase.

"The Fords were the first really safe cars that I ever drove. Those were some of the best racin' days of my career. God, we had some real racers then. Them days are gone forever."—A.J. Foyt

"The car was absolutely flawless but the only thing that worried me was that A.J. had only ten laps of practice before the race. For this type of event, that's not enough."—Dan Gurney

Bruce McLaren and Mark Donohue were instructed to lap at a 3:31–3:32 pace. This car always ran in the first six positions and was as high as second place, but various problems caused it to spend too much time in the pits.

Gurney cruises in second place just 10 minutes into the race. Bruce McLaren can be seen a safe distance behind.

"I started the race from the traditional Le Mans start. I got a good jump on the field and decided not to buckle my harness until I got to the Mulsanne. At the end of the first lap there were three Fords and a Ferrari ahead of me and I began to concentrate on our race plan. During the first couple of hours you try to stay out of trouble while setting a fair pace."—*Dan Gurney*

Bruce McLaren runs comfortably during the first minutes of the race.

"I made a fairly careful start in the race, getting away eighth or tenth. After the first couple of laps I settled down to our team instructions. Our cars could out-accelerate, out-brake, and out-corner everything else—including the Ferraris. On the straight we were 20mph faster than anyone else."—*Bruce McLaren*

Peter Sutcliffe's Ferrari P4 leads the Gulf Mirage (14) of Piper/Thompson, the Ferrari P3/4 (22) of Guichet/Muller, the Ford Mk. IV (4) of Ruby/Hulme, and the Lola Aston Martin (12) of Irwin/De Klerk.

"Driving the factory Ferrari 330 P4 at Le Mans was a glorious experience and the P4 was a lovely car to drive. I was teamed with German driver Gunther Klass and we were the third of three factory cars. Our car was almost written off by Klass in practice. He had a huge shunt and I thought the car was going to be withdrawn due to the extreme amount of damage. Ferrari flew up a team of fourteen body and chassis builders and they completely rebuilt the car overnight. They did such a brilliant job that it looked like the car had never been wrecked at all. Our instructions for the race were to hold back, be consistent, and stay in front of the Porsches, which was no easy task."—*Peter Sutcliffe*

The two Holman & Moody Mk. IVs run together through the Esses. The Andretti/Bianchi car leads Ruby and Hulme. It was during this time that Andretti and Hulme, in these cars, both set the same lap record of 3:23.6, or 147.89mph. A number of problems occurred in these cars, necessitating several unscheduled pit stops. Due to these problems, these cars were never able to maintain the pre-determined set pace.

Bruce McLaren leads the Porsche 906 of Buzzetta and Schutz through Arnage.

Right:
The Gurney/Foyt Ford is on its way to breaking most of the Le Mans records. By the end of the race, this car had not only covered a record amount of miles (3,251.563 miles) but broke the race average speed record (135.483mph). This was 10mph faster than the previous record set in 1966. This car also won the Index of Thermal Efficiency.

The Gurney/Foyt car leads the Bucknum/Hawkins Mk. IIB and the Thompson/Piper Gulf Mirage through the Esses.

Left:
Lloyd Ruby takes one his excursions into the sand bank at Mulsanne Hairpin.

"I drove a Mark IV at Le Mans in 1967 and I got stuck in the sand at the end of the Mulsanne. There was a car in front of me that blew the engine and I hit the oil and went clear out of the ball park. The car went so far up into the sand that there was no way that I could dig it out. In fact, it took the track people two days to dig it out."—*Lloyd Ruby*

1967

Le Mans: Porsche and Chaparral Offer a Challenge

Below:
The Porsche 906 of Vic Elford and Ben Pon was seventh overall and the winner of the sports car class.

"I was invited by the Porsche factory to drive one of their 906 entries at Le Mans in 1967. That was my first year there, and I was lucky enough to win what was then the sports car category and finish seventh overall with my co-driver Ben Pon. Since there was no way that we could stay with the big bangers, our strategy was to travel in a pack and wait and see. I got a great start and was in the top ten going onto the Mulsanne. My first recollection of the Fords was when they and all of the other big bangers went bombing by me. I realized at that time how important it was for the smaller displacement cars to stay to the right and out of harm's way. I remember that the Fords were gorgeous and they looked like they'd be so nice to drive and so comfortable, too. Compared to the 906 they were so fast and looked so elegant."
—*Vic Elford*

Above:
The Spence/Hill Chaparral 2F was the second-fastest qualifier and ran in the top three for several hours. The automatic transmission finally gave out in the 18th hour.

One of the newest Porsche prototypes at Le Mans was the Porsche 910. This car was powered by a fuel-injected six-cylinder engine and was rumored to have exceeded 185mph during practice. This car driven by Jo Siffert and Hans Herrmann finished fifth overall.

The Holman & Moody Mk. IIB was driven by Roger McClusky and Frank Gardner. This car was involved in a huge crash that took out three of the Ford entries at the same time.

> "I don't think the Indy drivers in the Ford team enjoyed Le Mans too much. Foyt, Ruby, and McClusky had never been there before and McClusky raised a laugh when he asked why there were so many trees so close to the race course? Gurney told him that they were French safety barriers. By the time a car got through them there weren't any pieces big enough to hurt the crowd."—*Bruce McLaren*

Chris Amon teamed with Nino Vaccarella in one of the Ferrari factory-entered P4s. Amon retired in the eighth hour due to a fire.

> "At Le Mans in 1967, I really wanted to do well in respect to Bandini's memory. He and I had shared the wins at Daytona and Monza and I really wanted to put up a good effort . I was teamed up with Nino Vaccarella and we were running at a good pace. We were giving away 50 horsepower and probably 30 miles an hour on Mulsanne to the Fords, but our plan was to run at a good pace, pressure them, and hope that they broke. No one ever thought that Gurney and Foyt would finish, let alone win, so we just let them go. Ferrari thought that they would never make it half way through the night at the pace that they were running. I would have loved to have had a bet on that one."—*Chris Amon*

The Sutcliffe/Klass Ferrari P4 expired with engine problems in the 18th hour.

> "The Ferrari 330 P4 was a superb car. It was much better then the 289 Ford GT40s, but it was no match for the big Fords. Unfortunately the crew spent so much time on the body repairs that they didn't have time to check the engine and that was to be our downfall. We were running fourth when we went out in the 18th hour with engine failure."—*Peter Sutcliffe*

1967

Le Mans: Strategy, Repairs in the Pits

Below:
Gurney exits his car as Al Dowd is already at work refueling. Max Kelly watches from the pit wall.

"No one wanted to be associated with this car in the beginning. All of the Ford people thought we'd never finish. As the race wore on and it became evident that we were going to win, they all came flocking into our pit."—*John Collins*

Left top:
A.J. Foyt, Carroll Smith, Dan Gurney, and Homer Perry discuss strategy during a pit stop.

"The greatest race that Dan Gurney or A.J. Foyt ever drove was when they won Le Mans in 1967. By the time they finished practice for that race, the goddamned car was a disaster. They had both made so damn many changes on the car that the son of a bitch wouldn't even go down the Mulsanne Straight. Gurney and Foyt were both fiddle fuddlers and they couldn't keep their damn hands off the car. When practice and qualifying were over, I told the crew to take the car back to the garage, put it on the base plate, and set it up like it was when we tested it at Riverside, and fuck it, let 'em drive it that way in the race. Of course, they did, and we all know the result."—*Carroll Shelby*

Left:
After the 1966 season, Jacque Passino took over Leo Beebe's job.

"Passino was an excellent strategist on whom I relied constantly. He was an excellent man and he knew a hundred times more about this business than I did."—*Leo Beebe*

Bottom:
Mike Parkes and Ludovico Scarfiotti talk during one of the pit stops about their flat-out charge to catch the leading Ford.

"Mike Parkes and Ludovico Scarfiotti drove one of the finest races I've ever witnessed in pursuit of the Fords. They never quit and they gave it their all, putting up record lap after record lap in pursuit of the Fords. When they came in for a driver change after their hour-and-a-half driving session, they were completely wiped out. They drove that P4 to the absolute limit and no one could have done more."—*Peter Sutcliffe*

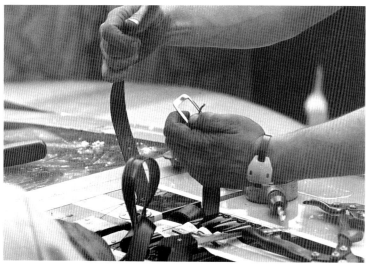

Previous page top:

Bill Eaton (left) and Dennis Gragg work to repair the deck lid of the McLaren/Donohue Ford.

"We had a problem with McLaren's deck lid at Le Mans in 1967. There were two concepts about how the tail should open. Holman & Moody said it should swing up from the rear and Shelby and Phil Remington said it should swing up from the roll bar. The Shelby method proved to be the best. As the car progressed through the race, the fiberglass deteriorated due to the high heat temperature and we began to get air under the tail and Bruce lost the tail at speed. In this case, the air ripped the tail right out of its mounts. The mounts were destroyed and we had to find the tail section out on the track. We dispatched McLaren and he found it and brought it back to the pits. We made some plates and riveted the tail down solidly and sent Bruce on his way. After a couple of laps, Bruce was called back in because Ferrari had done a protest regarding the tail not being able to be lifted, which is illegal. We cut the plates off and created two hinges, using the crew's leather belts, including Shelby's very expensive alligator belt. He couldn't really say no in front of the whole world. We laced the belts under the roll bar and through the main structure of the tail and the tail section swung open on the belts. The car did go on and it did finish fourth overall. That was quite a piece of work."—*Bill Eaton*

Previous page bottom left:

Is one of these belts Carroll Shelby's expensive alligator belt? Dennis Gragg took great pleasure in cutting off the end of Shelby's belt since he and Eaton only needed part of it for the repair.

Previous page bottom right:

Carroll Shelby catches a quick nap during a lull in the action.

Top:

Bill Eaton (in yellow) and Charlie Agapiou tape down the deck lid of the McLaren/Donohue car.

"This experience taught me that G.T. stood for Grey Tape."—*Bruce McLaren*

Right:

Gurney and Foyt keep up their record pace.

"When you're at Le Mans, you drive 80 to 90 percent, never 90 to 100 percent unless it's the last few laps and you have a chance to catch somebody. In those days you couldn't abuse the car for 24 hours. We didn't have the components that they have now, and the transmissions, engines, brakes, and suspension couldn't take that kind of punishment."—*Carroll Shelby*

1967

Le Mans: Gurney and Foyt Beat the Odds

Above:
Henry Ford (left) and Bill Innes show their approval of the race's results.

Left:
A.J. Foyt comes down to take the checkered flag. Foyt was heard to comment shortly afterward, "Did I win the Rookie Of The Year award?"

As Foyt drives to the victory stand, Dan Gurney waves to the crowd, Mike Donovan holds the champagne, and Crew Chief John Collins rides behind Donovan.

Right:
Dan Gurney and A.J. Foyt celebrate their all-American victory. An exhausted Mike Parkes is at the far left.
  "That win at Le Mans was a great win for me, Gurney, and America. Winning Le Mans and Indianapolis within a month of each other was one of the highlights of my career."—*A.J. Foyt*
  "I was very proud of our all-American victory because nobody expected Foyt and me to finish, much less win. We were voted 'Least Likely to Succeed.' If we'd bet on ourselves with the English bookies, we could have both retired after that race."—*Dan Gurney*

Porsche race team manager Huschke von Hanstein hugs Carroll Shelby in congratulations for his overall victory.

index